W.I.S.D.O.M.

Wonderfully Inspiring Stories

by a

Dominant and Opinionated

Mother

By Elizabeth Glotfelty

P. R. Glotfelty LLC
Cincinnati, Ohio

W.I.S.D.O.M. is a memoir. While some names have been changed or omitted, and events or dialogue compressed or recreated, this book has been a slow-burn catharsis covering twenty-plus years of internal drama and I feel a lot better having written it. Those who know me may recognize some of its contents, but don't worry, I'm the antagonist in this story.

Published in the United States by P. R. Glotfelty LLC

Library of Congress Cataloging-in-Publishing Data

Library of Congress Control Number: 2020921038
Glotfelty, Elizabeth.
W.I.S.D.O.M. Wonderfully Inspiring Stories by a Dominant and Opinionated Mother / By Elizabeth Glotfelty.
   p. cm.

ISBN 978-1-7360317-0-4 (hardback)
ISBN 978-1-7360317-2-8 (paperback)
ISBN 978-1-7360317-1-1 (ebook)

First Edition

10 9 8 7 6 5 4 3 2 1

Dedication.

Sookie, I hope this will set your mind at ease that yes, you will be a cool mom and a force that no toddler tantrum can tear asunder.

Just remember, treat them like they're a second-born and you'll be fine.

Table of Contents.

Introduction.

Many parent-centric books can be broken down into the following themes:

(i) they champion "babies are the best things ever!" to the point where thinking differently deems oneself a sociopath;

(ii) they feature endless examples of hyper-devoted mothers who drop everything and immediately run to their respective children but then wonder why they're perpetually exhausted and simultaneously amazed their children can't function independently;

(iii) the subject mommy tries hard to seem funny and honest about her adorable child-rearing quirkiness but the entire rendering is about as edgy as a pleather jacket from Ann Taylor; and

(iv) raising children as narrated by mature mothers who already have satisfying careers and livelihoods and who can afford to set the cruise control for a few years while they heavily parent their children to high-caliber success.

But what about the mothers who didn't have aspirations for parenthood? Or the women who don't see motherhood as fulfilling an innate need? Or those who are still trying to build personally satisfying lives and actual careers for themselves? Or the desperate souls who believed that having a baby would be the penultimate experience, but wake up to find out they have lost themselves to this new stage of life? Or the mothers who actually wanted children but realize their ratio of work to enjoyment is vastly one-sided and feel like dejected failures?

This book is for those forgotten mothers.

While there are far better books out there written by well-pedigreed individuals who have successfully guided children into adulthood, I am not one of those people. The jury's still out on Child's[1] self-determination and resultant adulthood. But as someone who didn't go to an Ivy, who spent the first five years out of college flailing between retail jobs and young parenthood, and who emerged into a semi-fulfilling career with relative personal satisfaction, I think I can speak to mothers who feel like they're not finished growing yet. I am one of you.

This book is not intended to dismiss those who feel differently. And this is not intended to diminish the rewards that parenthood and children can bring. The most rewarding relationships and accomplishments come from difficult and persistent efforts, children included. Besides, without the anonymous mommy-types mentioned throughout my book, I never would

---

[1] Throughout this book, I will refer to my child as "Child" and husband "Husband." I personally find it distracting and slightly annoying to read a parenting-related story that constantly refers to children by their names. (The fact this annoys me is the reason why some may find it odd I am writing a book that centers around, yes, parenting and children.) I end up getting distracted throughout the book and then completely miss whatever the author is trying to convey. I want to spare you from that, but I also recognize it may prove triggering every time you read or hear "child" or husband" in other sources. Although that may be a good thing for me, because now you will associate my book every time you hear Child or Husband and want to buy another copy for your friends.

have been able to monetize my grievances in this format. Thanks, mommies.

This is the book I wish I had read while pregnant or parenting a young child and trying to simultaneously grow myself. When thinking about what I ultimately wanted to convey in this book to those women who feel as I did during this stressful life stage, I came up with:

- You are not alone
- Others feel this way
- You can still pursue your goals
- You can use your talents and long-term focus to raise your kids the way you want

And then I thought, *I would never read that.* That was way too emotional. And that would never stand out from the glut of saccharine mommy tomes already on the market.

Parenting is a job. And it's perpetual. Reject the false façade of The Happy and Fulfilled Mommy. Tell me you don't see the need to approach this stage with a mix of humor and resolve. You are a dedicated and hard worker; you will succeed in this just like you aspire to succeed in other areas. Leave the sugary sweet mocktail for the others. This, ladies, is your bourbon on the rocks. And life is better with a bourbon or two guiding you through.

Acronyms, Acrostics, and other Mnemonic Devices.

Many mainstream books purport to demonstrate universal truths, but at what expense? Some leave little room for individuals to insert their own creative spin into the tale. Or inhibit a bespoke application. Instead, demonstrate to those around you that you have been gifted with the wisdom of the sages through the use of clever mnemonics. Mnemonic devices have been imparting wisdom for thousands of years and persist throughout all levels of society. Effective? Yes. Weird to write an entire book using this? Probably.

To reluctantly proliferate an already overused corporatism, let's level set on the terms I'm discussing in this chapter. To help with this, I've provided definitions below:

Mnemonic (adjective) [2]

Pronunciation: mne·mon·ic | \ ni-ˈmä-nik \

Definition:

1: assisting or intended to assist memory

2: of or relating to memory mnemonic skill

Acrostic (noun) [3]

Pronunciation: acros·tic | \ ə-ˈkrȯ-stik , -ˈkrä- \:

Definition: a composition usually in verse in which sets of letters (such as the initial or final letters of the lines) taken in order form a word or phrase or a regular sequence of letters of the alphabet

---

[2] "Mnemonic." *Merriam-Webster.com Dictionary*, Merriam-Webster, https://www.merriam-webster.com/dictionary/mnemonic. Accessed March 1, 2020.

[3] "Acrostic." *Merriam-Webster.com Dictionary*, Merriam-Webster, https://www.merriam-webster.com/dictionary/acrostic. Accessed March 1, 2020.

Acronym (noun)[4]

Pronunciation: ac·ro·nym | \ ˈa-krə-ˌnim \

Definition: word (such as *NATO, radar,* or *laser*) formed from the initial letter or letters of each of the successive parts or major parts of a compound term; also : an abbreviation (such as *FBI*) formed from initial letters : INITIALISM

Backronym (noun)[5]

Pronunciation: / ˈbæk rə nɪm /

Definition:

1. an existing word turned into an acronym by creating an apt phrase whose initial letters match the word, as to help remember it or offer a theory of its origin.

2. the phrase itself.

---

[4] "Acronym." *Merriam-Webster.com Dictionary*, Merriam-Webster, https://www.merriam-webster.com/dictionary/acronym. Accessed March 1, 2020.

[5] "Backronym." *Dictionary.com Unabridged*, Dictionary.com, https://www.dictionary.com/browse/backronym. Accessed March 1, 2020. Merriam Webster online doesn't have the term "backronym" in its listings, but it's an equally awesome mnemonic device that I use, so I've found the definition from a more egalitarian source.

Clever acronyms and acrostics bring joy to my life. I've learned after uncovering old writings from my high school days that I've always had an affinity for acronyms. There are dozens of us not-so-closeted nerds, even in Congress. Just look at the CAN SPAM Act of 2003. Effectiveness of the actual law aside, you know exactly what the intent is: manage and remove commercial spam email.

While attending law school, we were taught both common acronyms and further encouraged to reduce critical elements of a subject into easy-to-digest pieces. The quicker the recall, the quicker we could regurgitate the information onto our exam essays. The common acronym for adverse possession[6] that we learned in our first year ("1L") real property class was OCEAN: Open, Continuous, Exclusive, Adverse, and Notorious. I modified this acronym further to include "taxes" as paying taxes was an element of showing adverse possession in some jurisdictions and I thought "O CEAT" (pronounced

---

[6] "Adverse possession" is a way to gain legal title to a piece of property. "Adverse possession." *West's Encyclopedia of American Law, edition 2.* S.v, https://legal-dictionary.thefreedictionary.com/ adverse+possession. Accessed November 11, 2020.

"oh shit!") was an appropriate exclamation if one's property had actually been taken.

My current employer and Husband's former military employer also liberally applied acronyms. Unfortunately, many of these acronyms are simply words that are technically pronounceable, but they don't elicit the quiet appreciation that meaningful *actual word* ones do. For example, the Post Exchange, called "the PX," which I affectionately referred to as "the pixie," has no real meaning in and of itself as an individual word; it's basically a store on the military installation that could be used to purchase alcohol on a Sunday in a dry county. Although I did find an oddly fantastic pair of gold heels that I still have, over ten years later.

Likewise, the mnemonics in this book have been perfectly curated to convey key principles of advice for three specific areas: (i) advice for new and expectant mothers on themselves as an individual; (ii) advice for mothers on principles for raising their children; and (iii) training to use directly with their children. These are not all of the acronyms and acrostics that I've developed, just the ones that I believe are the most universally applicable. Own them. Improve them. Be inspired by them.

Now that we've established the basics, let's celebrate the clever cheat of receiving wisdom in palatable morsels and continue.

CHAPTER I
E.G.O.I.S.M.

As a new mother in my twenties, I tried desperately to hide the fact I was part of the maternal persuasion. Maybe my insecurity derived from driving a tan Mercury Villager minivan with a pink and orange racing stripe during high school. From my parents' perspective, passing on a fully owned car for the dual purpose of allowing (i) the newly licensed teenager to drive, and (ii) a parent to upgrade their own personal vehicle, was absolutely the practical choice. Unfortunately for me at the time, a pink-orange striped minivan, coupled with a *Martha Stewart Living* subscription, and a benignly nice girl persona pegged me as a future soccer mom. Why should I be so bothered by this? Because I knew I was not what others were telling me I was. Future children were never part of my identity.

If this were a counseling session one would quickly key into the fact that even from my earliest childhood memories, I had no interest in children or having motherly tendencies. I think my own mother recognized this early on as I was not forced to change diapers or watch my siblings, despite being the oldest child of five.

A significant clue to this hypothesis may be the fact that I did not have or like baby dolls when I was younger. Baby dolls were impractical. They provided no mutual engagement, only responsibility to pretend to feed, burp, and change diapers (fun!). No, I loved Barbies. Barbies showed me that someday I too would have boobs and independence.

When my best friend and I would play, we would create elaborate social situations filled with ensuing dating drama, complex family relationships, and fantastically diverse wardrobes, although the careers of my Barbies may have been more attuned with waitress and socialite thanks to the lack of powerful female characters on TV. As a natural brunette, I maintained solidarity with my brunette plastic sisters by positioning my Courtney doll (who for those who may not know, is the brunette best friend of Skipper, Barbie's younger sister) as the one to have a boyfriend, while Skipper was relegated to the third wheel. Every day was a new scenario and a new escape into future adulthood.

During adolescence, having siblings two to eight years younger than me further contributed to my negative perception of children interfering with my desire for independence. Family activities took the populist view of skewing to the lowest common denominator. I knew no other high school peers who frequented Chuck E. Cheese on a Friday due to the obligation of a family outing designed to keep the younglings occupied. For years I thought I was an introvert, when in fact I was actually a closeted extrovert due to my unwillingness to engage in child-centered activities.

When I was of the age to babysit externally, rational me would jump at the chance to earn some cash under the table. Unfortunately, I didn't quite have that spark compelling children to beg their parents to have me over again (though I tried). I can probably count on one hand the number of times I babysat growing up. Clearly compensation based on the infinitesimal amount of nurturing I could manage would yield poor results. Instead, I turned to earning money by making the most of my Midwestern farm genes with good old-fashioned yard work.

Reaching adulthood did not change past predilections. As an adult, I never experienced baby fever. Granted, getting pregnant at twenty-five really doesn't leave much time to pine for a child. You recall, dear reader, a common stereotype of a young female's progression into baby fever goes generally as follows: First, marriage; the desire to nurture the newborn marital relationship quickly supersedes and distracts from other priorities. Second, within two to three years (depending on the age the marriage occurred) early signs of baby fever begin to emerge. A puppy or other animal is purchased to flatten the baby curve and prolong childlessness. Finally, despite loving the precious puppy, the puppy is deemed inadequate and the female proceeds to absolutely need a baby yesterday.

As I entered adulthood, I had wanted to find A Special Someone and get married while young. However, this is where my preferences diverged from the stereotypical model; having kids was not the next step that I was envisioning so soon after that milestone.

I will concede that within a few months of getting married, I was absolutely dying for a puppy. I don't know where this desire came from. My family had one dog growing up and I never considered him mine or even paid any particular attention to him. Regardless of the source of this desire, I knew within a few months after marriage that I needed a puppy. And not just any puppy—a fennec fox eared, small-bodied rascally puppy that I would name after one of my favorite Star Wars characters.

Precious Puppy was only two pounds when we bought him. Puppies that small need to eat regularly in order to not succumb to hypoglycemia. Unfortunately, he was a picky little bastard. We found this out when he refused to eat dry food set out for him because it did not include wet filler. The following morning, Husband went to open the door to the laundry room, where Puppy stayed at night. As the door swung slowly open, he realized he was pushing Puppy's hypoglycemic and nearly comatose body across the floor. He yelled up to me in a panic, as I was still in our room, and for the next several minutes, sheer terror ensued as I frantically found whatever clothes I had lying around to get dressed. I bounded downstairs to help Husband try to revive Puppy by feeding him corn syrup to quickly raise his blood sugar. We rushed Puppy to the vet, sticky from the corn syrup and barely alive.

The next several hours of waiting and wondering whether he would live were the most stressful I had experienced up to that point. While he eventually revived, the sheer panic I felt during those few hours made me realize that I wasn't suited for motherhood.

Why would I want to put myself through this panic and stress trying to keep a child alive? The fun of having a puppy was quickly short lived given the realization of the responsibility that came with it. I questioned whether I would ever be up for or even want the challenge of raising a human.

Few of us feel ready for the ever-increasing challenges and responsibilities in life. Maybe this feeling of unreadiness is what helps us realize we can do more than the arbitrary limits we may be tempted to set for ourselves. Every new victory, regardless of how small, serves to bring us closer to who we could be when pushed past our comfort zones. This hypoglycemic event was, thankfully, Puppy's last. I eventually stopped living in fear that he would succumb again, and we continued to grow together, comfortable with this stage of life. But life doesn't care if we want to maintain the status quo. Less than two very short years later, you would find me changing Child's diaper two days home from the hospital and my mother commenting on how roughly I was handling him on my lap.

Life before maternity was stupidly simple. I understand that if some other traumatic experience (like the death of a spouse or a debilitating disability) suddenly came upon me I would feel the same way about my current life. Yet for all of the situational awareness I had regarding the amount of chaos children can wreak on a life, I failed to grasp what that truly meant. Indeed, life pre-Child was unabashedly all about E.G.O.I.S.M.:

Entertainment,

Grand aspirations

Other than kids,

Independence,

Selfishness, and

Minimal responsibility.

And I too, like all egoistic giants, was eventually felled by a tiny human.

CHAPTER II
Overcoming P.T.S.D.

What culminated into my **P**regnancy-induced **T**raumatic **S**tress **D**isaster began amidst a series of innocuous circumstances. Within six months of our young marriage, Husband and I moved to a military installation so that he could undertake a two-year specialty training course. While there, being naive and wide-eyed at the thought of what we could accomplish by the time we were thirty (spoiler: it wasn't that much), we decided to take an extended money management course offered by the military. We knew weaning ourselves off Uncle Sam's teat would come harshly, and we wanted to be prepared. And they offered free dinner, which meant a double bonus of saving meal money and one less night for me to hopelessly flail in the kitchen.

Several weeks into the course we had to document our financial goals for the next six months to two years. I distinctly remember surveying the room and thinking how much better place we were in than the others present. We were young. We were putting away (a little) for retirement. We did not have to worry about saving for a hypothetical child's college. We were ahead of the curve. The smugness was short lived.[7]

For those of you who are not familiar with military life, let me provide you with some context. This period of military living happened during the height of the War on Terror. And the only thing more prolific than camouflage on this installation was babies. Spousal anecdotes conveyed to me suggested this long-term training cycle was the only certain length of time that their spouses were consistently at home without the risk of deployment.[8] I completely sympathized with these spouses in the fact it would

---

[7] I still haven't learned from this Karmic experience and maintain bratty tendencies.

[8] Likewise, female members of the military who conceived would also allegedly get out of being deployed. But I didn't say that.

be nice to have husbands there to both impregnate and witness the ensuing birth. Several of my friends soloed in the latter, and I have the utmost respect and admiration for them to muscle through that experience alone. However, this is where my conclusion to the pregnancy hypotheses diverged from the majority. I followed this training school pregnancy scenario to the logical conclusion of deployment being inevitable. Therefore,

deployment + solo-parenting + trying to further my as-yet-to-be-determined career = a big hell no

Unfortunately, my fertility had another thought. (I'm the oldest of five children...What did I expect?)

I suspected an unintended pregnancy after watching the movie *Knocked Up*. More specifically, as Katherine Heigl's character slowly realizes that the onslaught of unusual symptoms she has suddenly come down with (errant vomiting, sore boobs) means that she is, indeed, knocked up, I was simultaneously coming to the same horrifying realization. I will admit that makes this Mother-to-be sound like either an idiot or severely lacking in independent thought, but it's the truth. Soon after the suspicion was established, I stealthily took a pregnancy test after Husband left for physical training[9] in the morning. Results showed definitely pregnant. I threw it away, left the bathroom and went downstairs to make breakfast while figuring out when to inform Husband.

Turns out, I didn't need to strategize too long because despite my long-standing practice of hiding candy wrappers under unassuming trash, I didn't stop to do the same to the pee stick. Husband came down to the kitchen, stick in hand, and I immediately burst into unhappy tears saying, *"I'm sorry."* Husband, probably too stunned to articulate, said nothing…which was probably the best response at that point. After all, he knows I'm no Mary and this is not an immaculate conception.

I barely had a few days to mentally prepare for this unexpected life change when Husband panic-blabbed the news to his entire circle of family and friends. So naturally I had to tell my family and friends before the

---

[9] Or "PT" as another example of a popular military acronym

concentric circles of Midwestern social life closed in and I risked offending my closest friends and relatives by them hearing the news second-hand. This is despite it being well within the first half of the first trimester window. Rational me would have preferred to wait to see things through for a bit more certainty before announcing.

Disaster Strikes

My P.T.S.D. incapacitated my mental and physical well-being. I will fully admit things may have been different if I had felt like a normal person while pregnant. Or had become so assertively high maintenance (with the disposable income to match) to temporarily mask the discomfort I felt for that time period. Instead, my body fully rejected this intrusion on personal autonomy and proceeded to lose its mind.

Society tends to infantilize women, especially during pregnancy. Tired tropes of craving pickles and ice cream or mildly inconvenient morning sickness that conveniently goes away by 10 a.m. can be found everywhere. This vastly underrepresents what is happening to our bodies for a period of 2+ years (yes, years, because the fun doesn't stop post-delivery). We veteran mothers need to tell it how it is.

Each pregnancy experience is different. And while I admire those with a glass half full approach, it also makes me want to dismiss anything they say due to a lack of situational awareness. Now, there is a line between honesty and gratuitous complaining. Complaints should have a purpose, whether for catharsis or driving action to change the situation for the better. This is related to the "make solutions not problems" advice that I address in Chapter V be SM.A.R.T. Complaining for the sake of complaining just makes one insufferable. For me, I need to acknowledge the uncomfortable situation so I can analyze what needs to be done to remedy it. Being honest about the physical, mental, and relational issues happening at this monumental period of life is the only way to help some of us get past it.

Not having an initial outlet or a mentor to help reconcile the situation of a surprise pregnancy with the life goals I had been concurrently pursuing, arrested my ability to move on. I did try to go out of my way to find some positive aspects to that certain pregnancy condition. Unfortunately, whether due to poor googling skills or just the absolute trash vacuum of the internet in 2009, I found nothing useful. To encourage transparency and solidarity with those of us who do not sail through pregnancies on a glowing rainbow of peace and joy, I've consolidated my main pregnancy grievances into a list that you may or may not find helpful. After all, having low expectations means that you will rarely be disappointed with the outcome.

Dumb as a rock. Before podcasts became a global phenomenon, I read podcast-ish books about a variety of topics, such as origins of household objects, and checked out GRE vocabulary books for fun. Unfortunately, one of the first things to go during that nine-month interval was my mental capacity. I was a freaking idiot. While pregnant, I couldn't handle reading anything more complicated than Twilight and Harry Potter (although, to be fair, Harry Potter was fantastic, and I think J.K. Rowling has a nicely complex style. Twilight had none of those things, but it went down easy). Several years later, as I witnessed many of my eventual school colleagues become pregnant, I was truly amazed at their ability to string sentences together, much less maintain excellent grades during a rigorous academic program.

I believe I've regained my mental capacity since then, but I also can't shake the feeling that I'm just Dunning-Krugering myself.

Migraines. As if losing my ability to think wasn't enough, I started getting almost daily migraines. I've always been migraine or headache prone; I have inherited my mother's proclivity for severe migraines although thankfully the rest of my family genetics have remained relatively mundane. Unfortunately, there are a number of triggers—hormone changes, smells, fluorescent lights, stress (it was not a coincidence that every school exam period included at least one debilitating migraine) and lack of eating or drinking fluids at regular intervals. Before you begin to question why I did not more actively prevent passing on this genetic pool of awesomeness, I will say that I have learned to successfully manage my migraines over the years so that they only happen once or twice a month and am otherwise a productive and contributing member of society.

Since pregnancy is a nuclear bomb for hormones, I eventually got a prescription to diminish their frequency and severity. While my doctor assured me that this was apparently safe to use during pregnancy, it did come with the possible side effect of inducing withdrawal symptoms from Child post-birth. Deciding that dealing with a withdrawal baby would indeed be my death knell, I eventually forewent the prescription and tried every other reasonable method available to me to reduce my discomfort.

I felt fat. By my estimates, at least 80% of white upper middle-class females have struggled with eating disorders at some point in their life. Another 15% were so blessed that they didn't have to worry about common things like poor genetics. The remaining 5% legitimately lived their lives in rejecting the arbitrary and meaningless standards inflicted by the media and society.

Thanks to the aforementioned failed internet searches, when trying to find some positive aspects during this disruptive time, every list of top ten reasons on how to "love being pregnant!" included being able to "eat for two." Being a staunch 80%-er, the uninhibited weight gain I experienced was the exact opposite of what would comfort me during this critical time.

Physically, I tried to stay relatively unaffected. Before pregnancy I had wanted to attempt a marathon but had not yet taken concrete steps to prepare. During pregnancy, running became futile. I felt like I had to pee the entire workout and was so sluggish that my usual pace took the same amount of effort of an all-out sprint. I switched to weightlifting, indoor biking and waddling, I mean walking. I tried very hard to eat normally but my immediate need to feed triggered exactly every two hours. Nothing could stop this feeling of imminent starvation. Despite trying to work out and eat sensibly I still gained forty pounds. And no, in case you're wondering whether this is a stealth humble brag on my pre-pregnancy body not having enough fat or nutrients to support a growing baby, it is not. I was far from underweight before this happened. I couldn't even use resource hoarding as a reason why my body would stop at nothing to get its next fix.

Desperation set in during a particular week at the end of my third trimester where I believed that I had exercised and eaten well. This belief was supported by constant pangs of hunger and my unscientific theory that Child would just start living off my fat stores for the remaining three weeks in utero. After arriving at the doctor's office for the weekly weigh in, the scale read that I had gained six pounds. Six. Pounds. And a constant feeling of starvation. I decided that from now on I would throw all caution to the wind and get the full whip at the coffee shop that just recently opened up on the military installation.

If you are reading this while pregnant, please add this next bit of unsolicited advice to the dozens of other examples you will receive over the next year. Being now older, wiser, and exceedingly more high maintenance, I highly recommend that you do whatever you need to do to look and feel your best during and after pregnancy. Your mental health will thank you.

Inopportune haircut. I made the mistake of cutting my hair while pregnant. Coupling that error with a forty-pound weight gain evenly dispersed to my face and ass, the association of cutting my hair during this time has scarred me ever since. I went into the haircut with no ulterior motive other than freshening up my look. My expanding midsection made me feel about as dead sexy as bloated highway possum.

Logic suggests that hair can't be cut longer, so any change would, naturally, be shorter. Unfortunately, my Twilight-saturated brain couldn't connect the circumstances to recall the long running stereotype of the pregnancy mom-cut-right-of-passage. You know the implication: long hair on a woman is a traditional signal of youth and beauty, such youth being felled by the responsibility of motherhood and burgeoning eyebags. Sweet, innocent young me, I still was naively assuming things would remain relatively unchanged.

I decided to try a long bob (a "lob," if you may, which also happened to be a prescient portmanteau of how underwhelmingly attractive I felt at the moment), cut to fall a few inches above my shoulders. I perceived this length to be both practical and chic; able to be gathered into a short ponytail for the days I couldn't style my hair.

Unfortunately, I made several miscalculations. First, that the effort of styling my hair wouldn't be thwarted by the Southern humidity. Second, that this unfortunately timed change would not be taken as acquiescing to the mom-cut. This latter miscalculation quickly became apparent when (no exaggeration) every quasi-friend I encountered immediately asked about my hair cut. "*Oh, you cut your hair, getting ready for baby, huh?*" "*Got the mom cut—it's official!*" I wasted no time quickly regrowing my hair and taking other calculated measures to show that I still got it, like wearing high heeled shoes to the grocery store. The P.T.S.D. lasted long with this occasion; I didn't cut my hair short again (even with postpartum hair loss) for several years.

Mitigating Disaster

Despite the many failed attempts of improving myself and my circumstances during the pregnancy, I did emerge with one long term win. Some parents prepare for a new baby by doing things like nesting, securing dangerous places in the house, or getting their finances in order. I, on the other hand, decided to stop washing my hair regularly.

I had read that you can train your hair to produce less oil if you don't wash it as often. At that time, I washed my hair daily. The natural course of action would be to adjust to washing my hair every other day, then eventually extend the intervals even further if needed. I decided to also start the experiment right away. I presumed that beginning while still pregnant rather than delay until after the birth would help me determine if the hypothesis is even correct. I'm no scientist, but it seemed reasonable to assume that variables such as postnatal hormones, disruptive sleep patterns, and atypical activity levels could skew the results.

I quickly surmised there were other initial hills to overcome during this effort. My head is slightly flat in the back, due to either remaining in the birth canal too long or not having enough tummy time as a baby. Regardless of the cause, the flatness of my head is noticeably exacerbated with day-old hair. Couple that deformity with an ill-placed cowlick at a top corner on the hair plane. When exposed, the cowlick makes it appear like I have an eye peeping from the back of my head. As you can see, I have a critical need for careful hair maintenance and this experiment was very risky by first world standards.

As scientific-minded as I tried to be, sadly I kept very few records. And I failed to consider one of the biggest factors of all: summertime in the South. It became impossible to tell if the extra shine wasn't from constant sweat or my hair acclimating to the lack of washing. At the end of my dirty hair experiment, results were inconclusive. Nevertheless, I decided my hair looked tolerable enough. So, with a spritz of dry shampoo plus a little extra backcombing, I stayed with the practice. Ten years later, I'm still on a two to three times a week wash cycle. Averaging ten minutes a week, to account for shampoo plus additional style time, I've estimated to have saved over 100 hours of wasted effort. Financially, I've estimated that additional savings of not using as much shampoo and conditioner has been offset by increased spending on dry shampoo and hairspray, so all in all, it's likely a wash.

Disaster Recovery

Some readers may find this entire chapter evidence that I am exceptionally weak. You are correct. I will fully admit that I have less tolerance than the general public. Moving on from a traumatic disaster takes time and learning how to live in the abnormal-new normal can be deeply unsettling. I struggled for five years to become even remotely comfortable with the fact that I had a child. Motherhood was such a hard adjustment that Husband for years later referred to that period as my continuous postpartum depression.

But disasters and the ensuing aftermath can be a way of redirecting our lives in a deeper and more meaningful way than if we had remained unchanged.

For me and many others, pregnancy and parenthood provided a window into the realization that we must be realistic with our priorities and ambitions. Most aspects of pregnancy can't be controlled, and no amount of wishing things were different can rectify imbalances.

We may not be able to accomplish a goal in the original timeframe we set for ourselves or undertake it with the expertise or ease that we had envisioned. That's ok. We still push through. But at the same time, while I can give myself a break in not performing to the level I had hoped, I can also use this opportunity to pursue goals I had never thought I could before. Parenthood raises the stakes of failure. Let's use this to our advantage. Harness the motivation to act with greater conviction than ever thought possible. After a disaster, a city can rebound stronger than ever. And so can you.

CHAPTER III
L.E.T. G.O.

When one thinks of sinister industries, one would typically think of health insurance, tobacco, or firearms. However, I posit that the baby industry is exceptionally insidious: take the most emotionally and physically vulnerable time of a women's life and make her feel even more inadequate. Most baby items are designed with the intent to exploit these maternal insecurities.

New and soon-to-be mothers can unwittingly succumb to the might of this industry through its calculated multi-front war using family, friends, and corporate marketing. How can an unsuspecting mother successfully defend against this onslaught?

Spoiler: it's nearly impossible. She may try, she may rebel, and she may win a few battles. But very few mothers can say they won the initial war. Eventually, after a few months or years when the dust settles and rebuilding begins, the occupied mother may finally wrest independence once she realizes half of the items she was told were essential went unused, and her house is overwhelmed with the spoils of good (and subliminal) intentions.

Fortunately for me, I was not exactly eager to have a child. So, when the time came that I had to start registering for baby items in order to get some help shouldering my new economic burden, I learned to **L.E.T. G.O**. and approached my minimalist baby registry with the following standards:

Is the item…

Legally required?

Endorphin enhancing?

Total crap?

Gifted?

Old but viable?

Legally required?

The car seat may be the only item that would fit into this category.

When we were acquiring baby items, knowing that said item would only be used for a brief time took the pressure off having to choose based on aesthetics or rugged utility. Those of us in the Midwest are very skilled with living with Good Enough so I tapped into that Appalachian endurance and curated my middle-grade merchandise. Knowing we would only have one child, there was no reason to go all out and get the best.

Newborn car seat was purchased, but a car seat-stroller travel system was not. My reasoning will be described further below in "Endorphin enhancing," but I knew even in the beginning that I would use other means of transport. Likewise, many baby registries advise parents to purchase an extra infant seat base for maximum flexibility. If Child had come along five years after he did and we were in fact both working, then yes. I agree. However, given that

Husband's job took him frequently away and I was not working, it was one purchase we declined.

While some multi-purpose car seats even covered the infant stage, I knew that the last hurdle I needed in my life was to forcibly upend a sleeping infant to put them into another contraption to transport them to our destination rather than remove via carrier. We made do with an infant carrier until Child became too heavy to adeptly fold into the car seat. After that, we bought an adequate multi-purpose seat that could triple as a mid-baby/toddler/booster seat. It was, as all baby related items we purchased were, sufficient.

Before we move on, kindly notice how short the legally required list is. And this list only comes into play if you must have a car rather than live in a chic urban environment where public transportation and good old-fashioned walking are du jour.

Endorphin enhancing?

Number one on this list and my first big purchase was a running stroller. I knew endorphins were going to be the only things that would keep me sane after Child was born. (I was still young and lacking in discretionary spending enough to withstand the pull of the ABV.[10]) Dozens of running strollers were evaluated and compared to determine maximum compatibility with my needs and goals:

First, price. There were a lot of high quality and name brand running strollers that would have been fantastic to have but buying new was out of the question due to price and personal use case. The 2009 trash vacuum did not have the same opportunities to connect sellers of used goods to buyers as there are today and our town at the time was not exactly a bastion of health and fitness, so bartering for a used stroller proved difficult. In the end, I couldn't justify purchasing an expensive stroller for just one child. As such, the moderately priced, better-than-average running stroller met this criterion.

Second, ease of running. I studiously poured over reviews to determine whether a fixed front wheel or swivel wheel was better for higher pace running and

---

[10] Alcohol by volume

overall run satisfaction (answer: fixed, even accounting for locking a swivel wheel into place). Narrowing down that preference reduced the remaining selection pool significantly.

Third, tear down. Since we were moving to an apartment, keeping the stroller neatly folded in the trunk of my hatchback car was the only realistic option to have no excuse to not get out and burn a few. I would need to be able to hold Child in one arm and adeptly set up or tear down the stroller with the other while standing in the apartment parking lot. Failure was not an option. And neither was successfully deflecting accusations of teaching Child his first potty words out of frustration with a wayward stroller. Impressionable young ears were at stake.

Fourth, weight. Running strollers can vary dramatically in weight, so I tried to find the lightest one I could. Between an ever-growing Child and Puppy riding in his own little space in the stroller undercarriage, weight would begin to increase dramatically over the next several years. Starting light meant I had more months of adapting to the increasing weight and still being able to run at a fast (for me) pace. Ultimately, the stroller I initially chose became the only one I used for close to five years. Five years is a long time, particularly in stroller life, and it still had enough life left to pass on to another family.

The second most important endorphin enhancing object I purchased was a baby wearing wrap. This wrap was a long piece of stretchy fabric designed to keep the baby in place on the mother's torso through a series of wrapping, tucking, and tying. I bought a baby wearing wrap since I am a fast walker and needed to quickly maneuver past persistent phalanxes of stroller moms.

In the ten years since I first purchased the wrap I've seen "baby wearing" become a phenomenon, which I get but at the same time the cult built around the practice is weird. Once Child reached around four months and no longer flopped like a limp flower, I ended up just carrying him in my arms like I was the reincarnated Greek wrestler Milo of Croton. I wanted to start reaping some fitness ROI[11] by carrying this figurative baby bull and building some chiseled arms and ass.

The final endorphin purchase centered on Child's own energy fix. As both Husband and I are active, I correctly assumed Child would likewise have energy to burn. When Child was around six months old, we purchased a baby walker, Jeep themed. The Jeep walker, although much more expensive than others, was not obnoxiously baby-themed as other similar products. Child looked like a bad ass as he practiced driving over our concrete floors, and we decorated the Jeep with local bumper stickers (such cool parents). Maybe it was nature, maybe it was nurture, but ten years later, Child is still enthralled with Jeeps we encounter while driving.

And that, my friends, is how we were inadvertently suckered by devious corporate marketers into brand loyalty straight from the womb.

---

[11] Return on investment

Total crap?

Also referred to as Superfluous Bullshit, this next section of items is basically a blatant money grab. My opinion on these things is likely to welcome disagreement and that's ok. But I still think they're stupid. For the record, I never bought any of the following items and have no regrets.

Wipe Warmers. Wipe warmers are incredibly frivolous. My reasoning: No child would be harmed by a cold wipe. This process was to be as unpleasant for me as it would be for Child. Child needed to learn resilience in an unpleasant situation. And I would not tolerate a high maintenance anus.

Video Baby Monitors. Honestly, I would rather use Child's nap time to forget my current situation and responsibility. A regular baby monitor was perfectly adequate and at the time, had the added benefit of still being within range for me to escape to the apartment gym to run on the treadmill. Mother needed to get as many endorphin hits as possible before Child woke from a nap. A second bonus to these old-school monitors: less appeal to hacking.

Diaper Pail Systems. I get the appeal. I really do. But I couldn't justify the added cost against the minimum efficiency gains, especially given the disparate product reviews. While Child was in diapers, we lived in four different places: a townhouse for three weeks when he was first born, an apartment with an outside trash disposal system, another apartment, and my parents' house. All of these featured a variety of floor plans and access to trash disposal. Despite how disruptive life was with caring for an infant or toddler, taking the trash out nearly every day did not add much to my regular routine. Not having to heft (or smell) a week's worth of dirty diapers down a few flights of stairs was well worth it.

Crib Bumpers. Crib bumpers may be aesthetically pleasing but functionally they substantially increase the risk of infant injury or death. I declined and stuck with a single fitted sheet in Child's crib to improve the ROI of my nine-ish months pregnancy.

Germ Barriers. Germs are a part of life. A cursory wipe and "vaya con Dios" was what Child got. Cart seat covers or self-stick table mats (although those are actually brilliant because they can be thrown away) were not anything I considered buying. To Child's credit, he timed his bouts of illness to occur on the weekends when it would minimally disrupt school or work schedules. By the time he was five years old his immune system ran on peak-performance and he has rarely gotten sick to the point of needing to miss school.

Swinging and Rocking Paraphernalia. Analyzing anecdotal evidence from (i) the 2009 internet trash vacuum and (ii) maternally experienced acquaintances, led me to determine that baby swings and doorway jumping contraptions were not items that I would welcome in my house. Not because of any safety concerns, but simply due to the high likelihood of Child hating them. Instead, we purchased a $5 reclining baby chair from the second-hand store at the military installation. Bleaching and washing later, it was completely adequate. This early assessment proved correct as for almost two years,

Child could not get on a swing without 1
his stomach's contents. Daily crisis averte

Gifted?

Related to the car seat were other items that aided the
primary directive of keeping Child alive: clothes,
diapers, and basic medical. For most of those, I relied
on the overzealous purchases of others for hand-me-
downs, whether it was clothes or rejected bottle
nipples. The latter I believe has directly contributed
to Child's situational flexibility. He adapted well.

Child made his blessed appearance three weeks
before we moved across states. Did Mother spend
time nesting to create a beautiful nursery for him to
enjoy during that interval? No, Child channeled sweet
baby Jesus and slept in a playard the first month of
his life. For all of the times that we used the playard
after those first three weeks, we could have done just
as well putting Child in a detached dresser drawer
instead, but we didn't have the foresight to know that
at the time and optically the playard seemed a bit less
judgey.

One of my favorite gifts I received pre-baby was an entire two-month supply of diapers in a plastic bin that later doubled as a toy box. The wise mother who gave me this useful and expensive gift will forever live in my memory. Her example continues to live on, as to this day I exclusively follow in her footsteps by giving diapers and wipes to expectant mothers. It's a beautiful gift for the expectant mother. The diapers will always be used. They won't take up space. They are appreciated for their purpose and then quickly forgotten.

Give shit or give things that carry shit. Which do you choose?

Old but viable?

In the spirit of reduce, reuse, recycle, let me posit that a baby room doesn't have to look like a baby room. Maybe the baby shower goodwill has run its course and function won out over décor. Maybe ancillary aesthetics didn't make the cut in your zero-sum budget. Maybe the thought of sitting in cutesy pastels for hours on end sounds like a torture cell. Regardless of the reason, let me describe Child's baby room so that you can feel warmly embraced by others who've been there.

Nursery themes have grown increasingly popular since 2009. Our theme for Child's nursery: Adequate. Recall that Child's first crib was a playard in a makeshift office for three weeks between location moves. Once we arrived at our new apartment, Child had his own room. Since we knew there would only be one child in our lives and we were trying to minimize expenses, we graciously accepted an offer of a used crib from Husband's aunt. The crib was twenty years old and perfectly functional, albeit with a few well-placed zip ties to fill in the gaps from misplaced hardware. Any potential risk to Child's safety with an old crib was mitigated by not having socially acceptable baby suffocaters (a.k.a. crib bumpers).

Let me paint you a picture of the rest of the room. First, our converted cotton mill apartment floors were stained concrete, which, while super convenient for cleaning, meant a bright green carpet (very cheap, thank you Ikea) was needed to make the floor sitting a bit more appealing. No baby rocking chair/gliders made it into the picture; I didn't see the need given Child's abbreviated sleep routine. (See Chapter IX P.A.T.T.E.R.N. for training Child to sleep.)

Income constraints and general desire to prioritize other areas meant we repurposed décor from our limited inventory. Husband had a prized Heineken shade lamp he artfully crafted during college, which sat at the entrance of the room. Back then it was a practical choice (we had a lamp and the room didn't have a central light) but appearance-wise we might as well have raised Child in a frat house. Someday, Child will see these pictures and wonder about what terrible parents we really were.

Running along the Heineken wall, we hung the family crest (purely contrived, no actual historical significance) to reassert the perception of grandeur onto the next generation. Other familial curse gifts littered the room because it was the best place to keep them: a Santa Bear (half of our family is from Michigan and I've never heard of this bear outside of this context); a cross-stitch picture of Noah's Ark from my babyhood; a plaque bearing the family first name; and a print of the Red Baron's plane. Across from the Noah's Ark, Husband's motorcycle helmet (a prescient addition given Child's future dirt bike escapades) was displayed on the bookshelf due to lack of space in the apartment elsewhere. The *coup de grâce* of the baby room was a framed print of the Outlaw Josey Wales poster hanging directly over Child's zip-tie crib. Who wouldn't sleep well with Clint Eastwood aggressively guarding them all night long?

Child lived in his frat house room for almost a year and a half until we moved to another apartment.

His bedroom in this new apartment was certainly an improvement—carpeted, now with a central light, and no longer a dumping ground for miscellaneous paraphernalia—in the same way that a postcollegiate apartment attempts to hide the fact that we still have no clue what we're doing but by nature of technically graduating, means that we should.

Soon after we moved, I walked into Child's new room one morning and discovered his still form lying face up on the carpet in front of his crib. I was terrified, even more so than when I had discovered Puppy's hypoglycemic body three years prior. Quickly flicking on the light, I bounded across the room and slid to my knees, lunging for him on the floor. I roughly shook him awake, which was the opposite thing to do if there was a suspected neck injury, but at the time I wasn't thinking of positioning him into neutral cervical spine alignment. Child sleepily opened his eyes and pivoted his head to look at me, confused as to why he was so roughly awakened. He was fine.

Once the heart-attack inducing moment subsided, I lowered the side of the crib so that he didn't have to scale a wall and blindly jump into the darkness when he wanted out in the morning. Then I started to think about crib alternatives since he had clearly outgrown his. I channeled my Depression-era grandmother's ability to salvage bread bags for supplemental use and decided to make do with the Ikea furniture that we currently had. Desperate to avoid spending on items that would only be in use for less than two years, Child's post-crib bed for a year was an Ikea Karlstad chaise lounge section piece pushed up against a wall. Coincidentally, it fit a twin sheet quite well.

L.E.T. G.O. of the temptation to get every baby related item you're told to buy. Chances are, the people or entities advocating for this blatant consumerism are getting something in return, whether higher profits or affirming their lack of creativity with sparse resources. If you later find that yes, you do in fact need a second baby changing pad for the playroom, the beauty of our commercial culture means that the item will still be there after the baby is born. Otherwise, L.E.T. G.O. of excess. L.E.T. G.O. of waste. Your future self will thank you for saving the time otherwise occupied with purging the house of baby items and instead filling it with meaningful activities.

CHAPTER IV
C.O.P.E.

We all have coping mechanisms. I drink sparkling water out of a champagne glass to tamp down on the potential alcoholism. Others may sign up for the PTA.

As a natural born cynic, I tend to immediately latch on to the discomfort of a certain situation. Although counterintuitive, I do this to help spin the situation into a positive light by remembering that things could always be worse. This enables me to see the positive aspects of that certain situation and be grateful for them, thereby making the present pain less acute. It's a quasi-depressing coping mechanism. I used this same coping method during the active listening exercise that Husband and I participated in during marriage counseling. For active listening, Person A first shares their feelings, then Person B summarizes what they believed they heard Person A say. After summarizing Person A's initial statement, Person B follows up with their response to A. Person A then must summarize Person B's follow up response and repeat the process with their own response. This is supposed to be a constructive way to work through a contentious issue. Unfortunately, the only way my cynical mind could remember this is to reframe active listening as fair fighting. Clearly, I'm no Pollyanna.

As new parents, we must bravely confront the first-world challenges we face every day through coping mechanisms and blind hope. When thinking about the positive side of having Child in my twenties, while that decade absolutely sucked with school and child-rearing, at least I got my body back via youthful metabolism and genetics. And when Child is out of the house and the pets have died off when we're forty-three, we'll actually have money to spend and still look hot doing it. On the other hand, if we had ended up having kids like normal professionals, well, of course the benefit to that timeline is having the professional stability to sustain a high quality of life during childrearing years and have the monetary means to get said body back through external help.

Naturally we all have different methods we use when trying to cope with a difficult situation. But regardless of the coping mechanisms we may individually deploy, the various strategies will have the resulting effect of either (i) helping us grow, (ii) allowing us to stagnate, or (iii) causing us to regress, as the stress-situation continues.

Personally, I want to use these stressful situations as opportunities to grow. As such, I've come to find the effective ways to C.O.P.E. with a stressful situation and encourage growth potential are:

Control what I can

Order my schedule

Perfection is not possible

Execute to move forward

Control what I can

There are several points in my life where I'm convinced the death grip I had on my schedule during that stress-filled interval was the only way I survived. It may not be healthy or sustainable, but at the time I convinced myself that I could do anything for a year. That year may have extended into another couple, but none were as difficult as the first.

Control is subjective. My bouts with disordered eating will attest to the fact that there are many ways I've tried to exert control in a period where nothing else was controllable. Parenting can be especially traumatic for control-freaks like me because it means you must relinquish any sense of control for a significant portion of your life. This is very hard to do.

I would not have considered myself very Type-A before parenthood, but that quickly changed with a child and subsequent career. While Husband was deployed for the first time, the multiple stressors of managing law school, parenting a toddler, and dodging mental breakdowns caused me to take extreme measures. Ceding any ground on my schedule and family life would have meant certain defeat.

My lack of control became evident within the first few weeks of starting law school. I knew I could not control the length and severity of occasional bouts of illness (Child or me). I could not control how other law students performed in my class, which would determine where I fell on the grading curve, and which further still would influence the type of summer internship I could achieve. But I knew that I could control my schedule. For nine months, I religiously followed a rigorous schedule designed to optimize academic and familial performance:

- 5:00am: Wake up, study for 2 hours

- 7:00am: Wake Child up

- 7:45am: Drop Child off at daycare

- 8:00am: Study in the library

- 9:00am-3:00ish pm: Class, plus more studying in the library during lunch break[12]
- 3:30pm: Pick Child up from daycare
- 4:00-6:30pm: Quality Child time
- 6:30-7:00pm: Dinner
- 7:30pm: Child to bed, dressed in the clothes he would wear to daycare the next day to cut out the middleman and extra washing
- 8:00-10:00pm: More studying
- 10:15pm: Bedtime[13]

Looking back at my schedule I'm more amazed at my ability to not watch TV during the week rather than wake up at 5 a.m. to study. It would take an act of

---

[12] I found another time-strapped mom in my class (who lucky for me was also much smarter) that I could study with. It was all study and no bullshit, which is something we both appreciated.

[13] The sleep tracking app I downloaded told me I could function effectively on 6 hours and 43 minutes of sleep as long as I went to bed before 10:30pm. It was 100% correct.

God to have this self-discipline again for a sustained period of time.

Although I've lightened up considerably since then, I still grapple with my attempts and failings with control. As one of my favorite sayings goes, nature abhors a vacuum. Control is a means to fill the void in our lives. Without control, insecurities take over the vacancy. I see this happen to me in a lot of places, but one of the most challenging areas to not project my own insecurities onto my child is through his relationships.

Child, being the perennial social butterfly, made a lot of close friendships in his kindergarten class. The following year he was assigned to a classroom without these same friends. I was deeply upset for him, although not upset enough to actually do anything about it—I'm not that neurotic. When I was in school, I was neither outgoing nor bubbly, so I had very few close friendships. I was in the same classroom as my best friend only a few times and those were special. I worried whether Child would inadvertently become left out due to lack of proximity. Thankfully, Child's gregarious nature enabled him to meet new friends. I hate to think that if I had tried to control his life, he would have missed out on new opportunities and new friendships. In the years following, he has continued to expand his circle of friends in new classes and with new friend combinations.

Today I continue to control what I can, whether it's cutting myself off after two drinks regardless of the social situation or rigorously updating my calendar to track and remember commitments. But tempering that effort of control with remembering "Perfection is not possible," as will be discussed later in this chapter, is the best way I have found to not succumb to paralyzing neuroticism if control ultimately falls apart. After all, we're unfortunately only human.

Order my schedule

At first glance, while order may look the same as control, it is not. There is a nuance between control and order. "Control" functions like an "if-then" statement: *If I control X, then I will get Y.* "Order" functions like an organizational tool to potentially achieve control: "*I am going to do X, Y, and Z today.*" Control invokes having some certainty over an outcome, whereas order is used to gain control by undertaking a familiar action, regardless of any ability to control the outcome. If life seems out of control, desire to order your life rather than control your life; the potential for personal satisfaction is greater.

For example, I have little control over how quickly Child can grasp a new concept in language arts, which is his worst subject. However, I can invoke order in his life to help him learn. Order can be found in prioritizing homework time, not allowing him to "multitask" during said homework, and (if time permits) reviewing the lesson with him to bring a different perspective outside of the Common Core curriculum. Order brings structure. And when the brain does not have to also analyze a new process introduced into the homework setting along with the homework itself, the brain can concentrate on actual learning.

When Child was Year Zero, I needed order. Control was not possible, but I thought establishing order in my life would allow me to cope with the continuous ups (rare) and downs (many) in that stage. Three months into parenthood, when patterns are beginning to get established but hormones are still raging and changing, I had what I would deem a late-onset postpartum depression. No doctors were involved in this diagnosis, as this is America and we use the internet and self-diagnosing to find and fix our problems. Moreover, this depression I was experiencing seemed new. I never experienced early-onset postpartum depression. I already knew things would be rough with a newborn, so with low expectations there's little room for disappointment.

Self-diagnosis complete, I began scouring the trash vacuum to learn about postpartum depression and determine whether it was even possible for it to start months after birth. Unfortunately, I found nothing. I resigned this atypical presentation of postpartum depression as yet another example of how I failed to fall on the center mass of the majority life experience curve.

Between moving three weeks after he was born and keeping Child alive during the first two months, I didn't have the luxury of introspection. But as keeping Child alive became routine, I began to clear the mental space to start to think about other goals that I had. Before having Child, I had thought about pursuing a few goals: going to law school and running a marathon (my mother is a prolific marathoner). Both were set aside once the pregnancy happened. I knew I needed another goal in my life and since I was unemployed and law school still felt unrealistic at this point, training for a marathon became the impetus to fill this void. Running was prioritized the same way as brushing my hair; some days may be more cursory but regardless of late nights or early mornings, regardless of whether or not the apartment was picked up, I made the time to pursue this goal.

This is not to say that my training was easy or perfect. I was slow. Running was hard. Injuries threatened to derail my progress. But I was consistent, and the training schedule became easier to manage by making it a habit. I used the hours to celebrate my small victories; eight miles with a stroller! Ten miles with a stroller! I pushed Child up hills so hard that my abs were sore the next day. The order and discipline that marathon training brought to my life helped me get through this postpartum depression period. Training was a way to sort through my frustrations and get that much-needed endorphin fix. Rather than feel like I was stagnating, I was actively working towards a goal that I had not yet accomplished.

My growing confidence with running created a waterfall effect where I gained clarity on other aspects of my life as well. Through months of training, I realized that I should not set arbitrary limits for myself. Training took consistency, deliberate action, persistence, and passion. Coping with my frustrations through running allowed me to grow into a stronger and more resilient person. I realized that maybe I shouldn't be so quick to doubt my goal of going to law school. If I could accomplish one goal, I could accomplish another. I am not that special, and these revelations are not unique to me. If I felt something was important for me to do, I could do it. Anyone could do it. All it takes is a first step.

Perfection is not possible

This is not a new concept, but I still need to say it: You are not perfect, and you will screw up your child in some way. You will. 100% certainty. Now that has been established, let's discuss ways to mitigate that impact on both yourself and your child.

Everyone has their different ideas of perfection. I never envisioned motherhood with rose-colored glasses. But I had culturally driven ideas of perfection: finding a group of like-minded moms; having a cute nursery; feeding Child organic and homemade baby purees; styling Child in coordinated outfits; finding satisfaction in motherhood. Yet, I had none of these things, and I thought there was something wrong with me.

The gratuitous pressure mothers put on themselves and the amount of disappointment we feel when we fail to meet those expectations could very nearly send a desperate, sleep-deprived mommy over the edge. The proliferation of social media promulgating hyper-organized parents whose respective missions in life seem to be giving their children the most idyllic existence imaginable has only made these feelings of inferiority more prominent.

That is why I am here to spread the Gospel of Good Enough. Good Enough is freeing. Good Enough is forgiving. Good Enough means that you did your best. And if Good Enough is sufficient for every mid-level executive to still get promoted despite minimal positive impact on their business, it's good enough for you. After all, they're getting paid more than you despite working fewer hours, so there's no need to kill yourself with parenting.

We don't need to be perfect to get ahead in any other segment of life. Motherhood is no exception. If perfection in everything is what we strive for, then we will be forever disappointed. And intolerable. So, I'd like to leave you with some of the things that I tried, and failed, and eventually got over.

Sign Language. When Child was less than a year old, baby sign language was all the rage. In theory it seemed like a great idea but in practice it actually took consistency and forethought. Baby sign language lasted for about a week. Child and I abandoned the attempt by mutual decision.

Breastfeeding. Breastfeeding for many women is a huge deal. Frankly, I don't see it as something that should be deemed the perfect solution to the question of what to feed a child. Child had to supplement with formula the entire time, so this may have contributed to my lackadaisical view on boob vs. bottle. For the sake of your sanity, avoid the B.R.E.A.S.T. debate (Being Ridiculously Enthusiastic About Swigging from Tits) as much as you can.

My approach to breastfeeding was the same as I took to nearly everything else child-related: *What was the easiest for me?* Sometimes breastfeeding made sense, but when I was out in public or left Child with babysitters, formula was my natural choice. Ultimately, I tried to mostly breastfeed (I gave myself six months-ish) because I'm both cheap and incredibly vain. After gaining forty pounds during pregnancy and literally working my ass off, why would I turn down the opportunity for a serious calorie burn? But regardless of money and weight loss, I knew that I would stop before Child started growing teeth and talking back. There were other hills that I would have died on when it came to breastfeeding. I would have stopped if it meant facing an elimination diet due to Child's inability to tolerate lactose or some other substance. I would choose dairy and not hate my life, and Child would get formula and not have an upset stomach; all win. Whether breast or bottle, it really doesn't matter and it's a really small thing to get worked up on.

Costumes. For the first six years of Child's life, I had a strict make-it-yourself standard for Halloween. It was not about money or vanity. It was to inspire creativity and not let poorly made polyester be all that one could aspire to be on that most fun of holidays. Eventually, I gave in to purchasing more costumes. Call it laziness, call it falling off the priority list, but the benefits of store-bought eventually surpassed my Martha Stewart aspirations. Ironically, the older Child gets, the more interesting his costumes become, so I feel reprieved for failing to resist the call of the Amazonian siren for a $15 banana costume.[14]

Execute to move forward

Not all ideas work. And not all situations are ideal. The important thing is to keep trying. At some point it's bound to get better. Or at least others will respect our tenacity.

You may feel like you've failed at times (and especially compared to the other super moms). But take a cue from your children when you're trying to get their attention: ignore distractions and keep doing what you're doing.

When Child turned ten years old, I attempted to show him pictures of myself at his age. It was then I discovered that I had none. My parents moved back to the U.S. during the first semester of my fourth-

---

[14] This banana costume was actually the subject of an interesting intellectual property dispute, <u>Silvertop Assocs., Inc. v. Kangaroo Mfg., Inc.</u>, 319 F. Supp. 3d 754 (D.N.J. 2018). Child's costume was created by the successful plaintiff, so it became a very educational purchase for me on copyright infringement. Inadvertent universal win.

grade year following several years of living abroad. Understandably, taking pictures and having birthday parties was the last of my mother's priorities during the move. She had five children, a house to buy, school enrollment, and her own sanity to manage. I haven't asked my mother about this time. She may well have blocked this from her memory, just as she has with many other stressful life events, we came to discover over the years. If I were to ask her, she likely would respond with a shrug and a pragmatic "well, there was a lot going on." Such Midwestern resiliency.

Maybe she perceived this as a parenting failure, or maybe she didn't. That was a time when people still had to take actual film to the store to get developed so they were much more forgiving on not documenting every generic part of the day. Today and every day, many aspects of raising a child involve unadulterated survival. That is normal and not a sign of failure. Following my discovery of The Year Without Pictures, I can confidently say I am not traumatized. It doesn't reflect any absence of love from my parents. I still have my memories of that year. And after all, I have documented evidence in third and fifth grade that I was in a protracted ugly stage, so I can only assume the pattern continued during the gap year and I am fine with diminishing that effect on my psyche. And even more importantly, I am still the firstborn which means that I have far more pictures than my siblings.

Before starting law school, I worried that I would scar Child for life by sticking him in day care and with babysitters. Part of this fear was driven by others' perceptions of day care, and some went as far to tell me so. But I decided to pursue law school anyway. And those childcare worries were unfounded. I did what I could to maximize the time we spent together, but otherwise trusted that it would work out. And as it turns out, children are incredibly forgetful.

Two years after graduating from law school, I asked Child if he remembered me being away at school and studying all the time. While he remembered my graduation day (not surprising, as there was a lot of cake involved), he did not remember the prior three years of law school. Not one. Today I am so glad that I didn't let my initial fears and guilt stop me from pursuing my goals. Now all I need to do is make sure I don't scar Child during the years he can remember so that he doesn't later seek the help of a competent psychologist who will undoubtedly uncover the psychological stunting he buried during my school years.

Challenges in life are inevitable. It's critical to learn to C.O.P.E. with those challenges through healthy measures, rather than by quietly standing over the recycling bin necking a champagne bottle to harvest the last drops of bubbly.

CHAPTER V
Be S.M.A.R.T.

When the blonde bobbed mommy at the playground tries to mom-splain that she took copious amounts of DHA to increase her youngling's brainpower and considers allowing her children to only watch educational shows on PBS as a point of pride, don't be intimidated. After all, you can distinguish between causation and correlation, and vitamins and television are no substitute for Mother's ever-compounding bank of life lessons. While child-rearing may be that mommy's life's mission, this is only one of many facets to yours.

From one reluctant mother to another, you don't need yet another person telling you what to do with your own child. A majority of this book is focused on my experience raising an (as yet to be determined) competent and capable child. But I don't want to infringe on your autonomy. You are, in fact, quite capable of utilizing science and common sense to rear a child. So as you continue on your journey with motherhood and its related endeavors, continue to be S.M.A.R.T.:

Start with yourself

Make solutions not problems

Assume you know best

Reject the script

Talk with honesty

Start with yourself

It's easy to fall into the trap of living vicariously through your children or your spouse. Even I find myself living vicariously through the opportunities Child has interacting with his grandparents. Young grandparents, combined with the economic freedom that retirement and stock options bring, means Child has a much higher fun quotient than Husband and I enjoyed as oldest children before our respective parents' peak earning years.

It's natural for us to want to give our children even better opportunities than we were afforded. Our society's long-held expectation is that our standard of living would rise with each passing generation. But sometimes these opportunities come at the expense of our own well-being. My time as a military spouse reinforced this latter point. At a baby shower I attended for another military spouse, the conversation among the spouses quickly devolved from personal reflections on the soon-to-be-mother into discussing what activities the attendees' husbands and children were doing. As the chatter delved deeper and deeper into mediocrity, I remembered wanting to ask, "but what are you doing?" Unfortunately, it appeared that there was indeed nothing else going on except their respective husband's careers and kid activities. I myself was also pregnant. And that scared the shit out of me.

Caring for yourself is not selfish. Everyone respects martyrs, but no one really wants to be one. Mommy Martyrs are women who forget that they themselves need to be nurtured. Mommy Martyrs have the mistaken belief (which is likely repeatedly enforced on multiple fronts) that they must sacrifice all to raise their children. Eighteen plus years (or make it thirty, depending on the number of children plus allowing for failure to launch), and congratulations! You've given it all! Mommy Martyrdom never appealed to me. After all, I must live with myself for the rest of my life. Children will grow up, leave the home and then immediately establish visitation boundaries and decide the ways they will never act like you.

Following their children's emancipation, Mommy Martyrs who had previously given themselves completely to their children are smacked with the cold hard realization that there is nothing left after the children leave. Career dreams are shot, they haven't changed styles in fifteen years, and they have no idea what they want to do with the next twenty years of their lives. All that is left is to continue the vicious Mommy Martyr cycle as Granny Martyr. And Granny

Martyr, try as she might, will never be able to ingratiate herself as the ultimate caretaker of her grandchildren without usurping their own Mommy Martyr. And that Mommy Martyr won't go down without a fight.

It's not easy to start caring for yourself. It can seem downright impossible to live outside of the immediate chaos of young parenthood. So be kind to yourself and let yourself know it. When you're feeling depleted, even small acts of self-kindness can add up. Think of one thing that will make your day better for you. Now think of three more. I'll leave space in this paragraph for you to do it:

1.

2.

3.

4.

If you're having a hard time making space while shouldering the burden of parenthood, go to Chapter IV Boundaries to build relationships. Or if you've absolutely run out of ideas, go to Chapter VII S.E.L.F. This stage isn't forever. Don't lose yourself during it.

Make solutions not problems

Despite the common foundations of ambivalence about motherhood and not wanting to lose one's personhood, not everyone who reads this book will come from my background and perspective. But don't let the principles that we've discussed keep you from doing what you can now. Excuses are the opiate of the masses. You make solutions, not problems.

Remember the chapter on how to C.O.P.E.—while one can't control outcomes, we can control how we process stressful situations. It's too common, whether in our personal or professional lives, to think of all the reasons a potential situation is unsolvable. But we're not quitters and we're certainly not common.

I felt incredibly frustrated in my mid-twenties with trying to determine what type of career I should pursue. Within a month of deciding to start studying for the LSAT[15] I found out I was pregnant. I didn't think that I could manage both law school and motherhood, so over the next year I did nothing towards pursuing a law career. But the desire to resolve the dissatisfaction I felt with perpetuating my current situation ultimately led me to revisit that earlier decision. That's right. I was so desperate to get out of being a stay-at-home mom that I wanted to start law school the same year my husband was deployed. I don't have the balls to stay at home.

I took action to make solutions for the problems I would face getting there: I studied for the LSAT while Child took naps. I started a part time job and studied during downtime. I asked for help from local "adopted" grandparents who were more than willing to help watch Child so I could study or take the LSAT while Husband was occupied with the military. Other friends offered to watch Child for a few hours to give me a mental break.

---

[15] The Law School Admission Test is the first of many toll gates potential lawyers must pass through, which are all designed to drive you to increasing levels of stress-induced psychopathy. If you succeed, congratulations! You're a lawyer.

It would have been much easier to convince myself that attempting law school with a young child and a deployed husband would be impossibly hard. Those three factors in themselves were all incredibly difficult life events. There were also multiple opportunities to back out of this pursuit. I was waitlisted to the school of my choosing and didn't have the flexibility to wait it out to the last minute to see if I could manage to matriculate, because I had to line up childcare ahead of time. To save my sanity, I decided instead to enroll in the other local school I had been accepted to. I also had the opportunity to spend a year abroad living with my parents (and permanent in-house baby help) and delay starting school. But I declined. Because I am secretly a coward. And I knew that if I didn't start when I had the resolve, then I would just make excuses. And if I somehow talked myself out of starting my career, then I would live with that disappointment for the rest of my life.

Maybe a problem that you're facing right now seems insurmountable. Maybe you have some control over it. Maybe you have no control over it. But are there areas in your life that you can improve or resolve that would make this uncontrollable situation more tolerable? Are there other steps that can be taken to get you eventually to where you want to be, albeit with a detour? Making solutions to problems you face encompasses two aspects: (i) addressing through action and (ii) changing mindset. If actions can't resolve the problem at issue, then we may just need to reaffirm to ourselves that this setback won't derail everything else we have going on. We can't let this problem infect other areas. Sometimes all we can do is mantra on repeat: "just get through it."

Assume you know best

Pre-parenthood, all of us had assumptions that post-parenthood would prove naïve, such as assuming a berserk toddler at a restaurant can be easily controlled. People love to assume others are incompetent. As a digital society, it's easy to find groups that echo the same assumptions that we do. In spite of this, it's also very easy to ignore those who believe differently; just close the browser or mute the ignoramus spouting off. The more difficult to manage are the cultural expectations that can arise from in-person interactions.

As someone without any family history involving the practice of law, I knew that I faced certain disadvantages approaching law school compared to others. To mitigate that disadvantage, during the first month of my 1L year I scheduled meetings with various professors to seek their advice on how to approach law school and recommended studying techniques. During one of these meetings, a well-meaning professor bluntly told me that I would not be able to make As. She did not know me. But she did know that a not-quite toddler, a husband deployed for a year, and a rigorous curriculum all competed for time and attention. I understood my professor's perspective; the economy was in the toilet, prospects for quality legal careers were very poor, and law school was expensive. But I also knew that becoming a lawyer was something that I truly wanted to pursue.

I assumed that I would succeed in law school. But in order to succeed, I had to maximize every opportunity to study efficiently, spend quality time with Child, and connect with Husband when possible. Without having a child, I don't know if my determination would have been quite as intense. Children force one to think with a broader perspective and act with a long-term focus, rather than concentrate on temporary pain. This larger perspective fueled my motivation to continue through the discomfort a high-stress situation brings. Ultimately, the professor was right. I didn't make all As. But I managed to do well enough to secure a competitive internship and set myself moderately apart from the overwhelming majority of my single and childless peers.

Assuming you know best about how to raise your child isn't a one-time matter. You will be challenged about this throughout your entire parenthood. When Child was five and I was a newly-minted attorney, I co-hosted a baby shower with my mother. Husband was away on his second year-long deployment at the time. One older, very well-kept attendee was making small talk with me. When I disclosed that I was a lawyer and Husband was deployed, she immediately responded: *"And you have a son? Where does he go when you're working?"* The facial expression going with her questioning implied that she thought he was left at home all day. I'm unfortunately not that quick-witted and am a much better writer, so I couldn't think of a reply other than say he was in daycare. The conversation ended quickly after. Another friend of mine (pregnant and a doctor who had faced the same incredulity for trying to pursue motherhood and a career) was there and we quickly commiserate on the ridiculousness of certain generational assumptions.

Please don't misunderstand—this advice of "Assume you know best" does not mean you should blindly forgo others' advice in favor of your own assumptions. We are all idiots in some (or many) ways. The painful realization of knowing "we don't know what we don't know" only comes from a requisite amount of experience or training. Seek counsel from those whom you respect. Weigh and challenge that counsel against your own assumptions, fact-checked by other sources. Don't be afraid to admit if you're wrong. Mistakes are inevitable. The more we can learn from them, the more depth we can bring to weighing our subsequent choices. And for the love of all things, just because it's on the trash vacuum, doesn't make it true.[16]

Reject the script

Reject the script followed by the typical mommy. When Child and his wild friends are running around and climbing over railings to get to an errantly thrown ball, I don't tell them to be careful. They'll just tune that shit out. A well-placed "don't mangle your testicles" gets more to the point (because who wouldn't rather deal with a broken arm than a punctured ball sack?), and has a bonus effect of gaining respect from other mothers within hearing proximity.

Reject the script of the culturally perfect mommy. In nearly every job I've had, even the less sophisticated, non-corporate ones, employees have taken psychological assessments to determine how we approach problems and where our strengths lie. Goals for these activities were to understand how we

---

[16] Unless it's this book. If you purchase this book off the trash vacuum, know that it has been well-researched and deemed completely accurate.

worked, what we needed to do to compensate for our areas of weakness, and how we could use the skills of other colleagues to strengthen our overall impact with the organization. None of these psychological assessments deemed one type of personality to be more perfect, or better than another, or force conformity to the majority.

Similarly, society has reached a point of understanding that children are, in fact, different. These differences mean that not all children can or should be raised using the same parenting tactics. When will society allow mothers to do the same with the way they parent?

In no other area do we expect individuals to conform to subjective ideas of perfection other than motherhood. Yet many still think that all mothers or parents should engage with their children the way culture dictates one should. I understand that some people may find sitting on the floor and placing circles into the appropriately shaped hole fun, but I am a parent that does not in fact enjoy playing most things with my child. As long as a child is physically and emotionally cared for, why should it matter? My earliest and fondest memories are not of my mother playing with me (with sequential pregnancies I don't blame her one bit), but of me playing with my friends or using my own imagination. Children can and should learn by playing by themselves and with their peers.

Last winter I received a text message from a dear friend seeking affirmation that she did not let her kids down with a lackluster holiday. This friend, with three kids ages six and under, spent the holidays hiking, going to playgrounds, playing with new toys, watching movies, riding bikes and baking. She felt guilty that she did not also take her kids to go rock climbing or to a trampoline park. What have we become as a society where we don't think all of the former examples of engagement are enough? Is it social media? Other parents? I wanted to immediately say, "*[insert very strong expletive here]* no," but my friend doesn't have a sailor mouth and seemed sensitive at the moment, so I refrained and instead gave a gentle response and affirmed what she had done was in itself amazing and beyond what any person would be expected to do.

Reject the script of failed expectations. Maybe you feel guilty that you're not doing family pictures this year. Or putting up outdoor Christmas lights. Or your child's first year birthday party would never dare show its pathetic face on Pinterest. Who cares? No one will. We are not as important as we think ourselves to be. So, don't spend one more second worrying about what you're not doing that others are.

And finally, reject the script of motherhood as sacred. Motherhood is important, yes. Motherhood is the hardest thing many of us will undertake. For me, an accidental pregnancy and parenthood exploited every ounce of personal weakness. But don't think for a second you can't make light of the absurdity it can wreak on a life.

Speaking of accidents, this is actually a great way to answer the typical interview question of: "*What has been a challenge in your life and what did you do to overcome it?*" Begin with "*Before the accident…*" and then move to describe how you overcame those challenges to get where you are today. Just don't mention that accident means pregnancy. Or do, and see if they appreciate your humor. If they don't hire you after that, you wouldn't have wanted to work there anyway.

Talk with honesty

Having baby experiences with others is a luxury. It's insanely hard falling outside of the life stage bell curve. Undertaking a severe life change is lonely and undertaking a severe life change while feeling socio-economically and culturally isolated on top of that is even harder. Having a baby at twenty-five in the military community might as well have been a geriatric pregnancy. While most civilians were still on their parents' healthcare, many military spouses were shooting off babies intentionally by twenty-one (and those were the officers' wives). I, on the other hand, considered three kids by thirty and the haggard disposition to show for it a Dantean nightmare. Unfortunately, the hormones pumped into the installation's water supply had a different intent (I'm only lightly joking...out of four similarly-situated, college graduate friends who were trying not to have a baby, only one of us came out of that two-year training unscathed).

In comparison, now we are living in a well-off (for the Midwest) community filled with forty-year-olds regaling us with their DINK[17] life war stories. Compared to them, we may as well have been teen parents. While Child is undoubtedly privileged, there is no way we can compete with a dual-working couple sailing on five to ten years of additional professional experience. Child, in his own mild way, is learning the importance of gratitude and Mother is learning the art of humility and candor when speaking to Child about personal finances and explaining for the tenth time why we are not going out to eat at restaurants on a whim or buying a Tesla.

Honesty can be intimidating. I tend to miss social cues that one takes for granted, such as providing an actual response to how I am doing when asked, "how are you?" rather than giving the generic, "good." But

---

[17]Double Income No Kids, as opposed to our experience of SUCK: Single-income, Underemployed, Cute Kid

I've found that being honest with others about your struggles encourages offers of help. Most friends or family are willing to support, but they need to know how. I have a rule where if someone makes an offer, whether to buy a coffee or watch Child, I take them up on it. My reasoning is simple: Either they want to help and are happy to further the relationship with my acceptance, or if they are not sincere and only offering out of cultural or social obligation, I want to make them regret insincerity and think twice the next time they feel tempted to blindly follow social norms.

My corporate mom friends exchange stories about how they continually fail their children, like not volunteering for classroom parent parties or not creating bespoke back-to-school signs and selfie stations in the front yard on the first day of school and posting the results on social media. I likewise engage, not to one up others' tales of failure, but to lovingly reassure them that child protective services can't arrest us all. There's a line between praising realistic mom experiences and engaging in a race to the bottom with perpetual "trying to have it all and failing" over both our professional and family personas. Take the position of extreme honesty and borderline selfishness when speaking about motherhood to other moms. Subversively admitting how one truly feels about certain aspects of this job and life stage is incredibly freeing.

CHAPTER VI
B.O.N.D.

There's a lot of pressure on mothers to bond with their babies. Many new mothers, still high from pain meds and unadulterated expectations, may feel strong emotions of relief, excitement, awe, or even love. But after the oxytocin surge has diminished and the new mother is starting to feel the excruciatingly tender ache of working nipples, the cautious sting of a traumatized vagina, or the helplessness of a c-sectioned abdominal wall, stuff gets a little less rosy.

Speaking to my own experience, when Child emerged, did I have an overwhelming feeling of love? Not that I could tell. Don't get me wrong, I was happy to see him. Mainly because it meant I was no longer pregnant and could start adjusting to life under the "new normal." Reaching the destination has always trumped the journey for me. You could say Child's and my first bonding experience was commiserating over our respective circumstances. It must have been a shock for a baby to go from a dark and warm uterus to a bright, loud, and brisk outside. How unpleasant and terrifying would that be? No wonder they cry like they do.

It's often taken for granted that bonding is easier for mothers than fathers. Hormonal magic aside, often it's because mothers (in the U.S. at least) have been the ones to traditionally stay at home for a time after birth. Thankfully, paternity leave is becoming more equalized and many fathers are also starting to take the entire leave period and not just a week or two. I am fully in favor of this. Fathers absolutely need an equal opportunity to bond with their young infants and get left behind in the corporate race during the succeeding months they stayed home to care for a child.

A baby's arrival is purely hypothetical until the blessed event occurs. Once baby arrives and the parent becomes Stockholmed by parenthood, one might as well make the best of the situation and learn to B.O.N.D. with their captor and stage of life by establishing:

Boundaries to build relationships

Opportunities to engage

Not everything is worth doing

Delegation of tasks

Boundaries to build relationships

Watching and silently judging others has qualified me to recognize certain personal boundaries that would never be crossed. Most of these boundaries derived from segregating the motherhood side from my normal, autonomous personhood. For instance, I determined that Child would not alter my music choices. Sure, I may turn to clean versions of certain songs, but relative genres with their original singers have stayed intact. No Kidz Bop here. I'd rather pierce my eardrums with a pencil.[18]

Boundaries are personal and don't have to make sense to anyone but the enforcer. A long-standing rule I have held from the onset of parenthood was that the first floor of any place I lived would have no toys in it. Since we moved five times during Child's first decade, this was subsequently adapted to apply to the main living space of an apartment, since we did not always live on multiple floors. Some may think this rule is crazy and impractical. But I knew myself. This rule was critical for my sanity. I would rather expend the effort to enforce said rule than try to unsuccessfully cope in a sea of unending chaos.

Child and I lived in a small, rectangular, one-bedroom apartment during my first year of law school. The apartment was divided, left to right, into three main areas: Bedroom, kitchen and bathroom, and living room. The main entrance to the apartment went

---

[18] I have it under authority from my good doctor-mother friend that "kids' music is actually tolerable with margaritas." So maybe just stick with margaritas to avoid rupturing your eardrums with a sharp object.

through the kitchen. The bedroom and the separately-situated bathroom had their own doors.

I determined the best way to enforce a toyless main space was to give Child the bedroom so I could shut his door. Most parents would probably consider putting both beds in the bedroom (ours was big enough to accommodate that), but most parents probably don't demand the amount of personal space that I do. My bed went in the living room; the next year would be nothing but study and survival. Husband was deployed. A burgeoning law career was at stake. Feng Shui had no place in a war zone. This layout worked exceptionally well, as I could shut the door and (i) seal in the toys or (ii) take a stress nap on the floor of his bedroom if life got too overwhelming. With Child contained in the same room, mischief and toys were managed.

Frequent threats of, and actual engagement in, toy purging also played significant roles to reduce the ever-present threat of house clutter. Exhortations to grandparents for experiences, rather than stuff, also worked relatively effectively. If you too decide to adopt a similar stance, just pretend that you're practicing Scandinavian minimalism, and no one will question your toy tyranny. They will instead be amazed at your ability to stay on-trend.

Don't be afraid to expand the practice of setting personal boundaries to include boundaries with the people you love. When Child was three months old, I started training for a marathon. At this point I was not working, so having the time and mental capacity to tackle this goal was completely doable for me. Husband's job kept him away from home three to four days at a time on a weekly basis. During marathon training I scheduled long runs (ten miles or longer) during the times he was home so that I could take a break from pushing a fifty-pound stroller.

On one of these particularly long runs, he called me two hours into my workout and immediately asked when I would be home. I quickly sensed the frustration in his voice (Child had been difficult and demanding during this last stint away), but any pity was quickly overwhelmed by red-hot anger. I immediately stopped running, which added to my anger because Husband now also blocked my much-needed endorphin rush and yelled into the phone, "you've been gone two days and I've been gone two hours!" I angrily mashed the end key on my cell to terminate the call and continued on my run. To his credit, he knew he screwed up and that is the last time he ever asked such an asinine question or interrupted a run.

Since that incident, Husband has been a champion of my Me Time and for that I am grateful. I likewise went on the offensive with Child. Certain boundaries were established early and forcefully in order to make this parenting situation work. Thanks to this early intervention, Child never had issues with being in a stroller or really going anywhere I took him. It's a similar concept to putting clothes on pets—do it early and often and they will quickly accept that this must be how things are.

Opportunities to engage

One of the things parents get excited about as children grow older is introducing them to activities we like to do, albeit the parental enjoyment factor of introducing versus doing these activities jointly depend on personal preferences for autonomy and efficiency. Likewise, a large part of bonding with Child has been to discover the things that excite him and do that new activity together. This of course gets obviously easier once they're verbal and can somewhat engage in meaningful conversation and activity.

My father loved baseball growing up and tried very hard to get my siblings and me to also play sports. Unfortunately, the spark of "ball sports" never quite took hold. In an act of desperation, he asked us what it would take to play sports. I replied, "pink and purple uniforms." This was before *In a League of Their Own*, so neither one of us had seen pink skirted uniforms in action. My father makes solutions, not problems, so when he questioned me again to see if I really would play under this potential solution, I gave a non-committal, "Maybe."

Why am I telling this story? Well, the other sport my father loved was basketball. And naturally, the only teaching that ever stayed with me in his quest to introduce the sport was the acronym for how to shoot a basketball: B.E.E.F. (Balance, Elbow, Eyes, Follow-through). What B.E.E.F. didn't teach me was to not kick my right leg back like a fool every time I shot the ball. Maybe if I had learned "B.E.E.F.S." (Balance, Elbow, Eyes, Follow-through, Stand still) then we'd have a different outcome. To conclude this story, despite best efforts, I never came to accept the risk of a ball to the face, so I just ran track instead.

All was not lost, however. Grandchildren are the ultimate do-over for grandparents. Child seems to have acquired all the natural athleticism that skipped a generation, so my father is now taking on a part-time job of personal basketball and baseball coach. My father is happy sharing a common interest with his grandson and Child is thrilled with the extra screen time from endless game play reruns. And I am contributing, despite my lack of ball-sport competency, by remembering the B.E.E.F. lesson taught by my father, and creating helpful acronyms to teach Child the intangible characteristics that sports require.

But lest we forget that we're actually dealing with parenting, engagement has a more negative connotation. This engagement occurs when there are two opposing forces threatening to collide. Later in this book you'll read highlights from the innumerable trips Child and I took to our local zoo. These zoo outings have remained some of the best memories we've shared between his ages of one and four. But not all zoo trips were conventionally successful. As Child grew older and started experimenting with temper tantrums, the zoo also became the ultimate tool for a power play.

The privilege of having a zoo membership coupled with a ten-minute travel commitment meant that it didn't matter if zoo trips were two hours or twenty minutes. The zoo was a fast and easy way to fill time and distract both of us. On one occasion, within five minutes of arriving at the zoo, Child started to throw a tantrum. A minute of Mother's gentle correction proved ineffective. Mother escalated to nagging with increasing fervor. Child responded by continuing to misbehave. Ultimately, Mother fired a final warning shot of threatening to leave if he did not immediately correct himself. Tantrum attack unwavering, Mother responded with a counter strike of leaving the zoo. Child eventually calmed down but not before learning Mother didn't deal in empty rhetoric. Tantrum engagement victory. To this day, our shortest zoo trip on record was fifteen minutes.

The zoo became a place to bond over our love for animals, build memories, and engage in parenting. Maintaining a personal boundary to only be at the zoo if we were both having a good time kept it as enjoyable for me as it was for him. If I had forced myself to stay at the zoo despite a tired or disobedient child, then it would have stopped fulfilling the zoo's purpose in my life. It would have become something to dread. Instead, Child quickly learned that engaging in poor behavior would result in leaving a fun place and this Mother does not give empty threats. I strongly believe following through has preempted many disruptions. Opportunity to engage, met.

Not everything is worth doing

Days are finite. For that reason, we must prioritize what matters to us. This is an individual assessment and comes with a high likelihood of guilt, especially when we see others achieving things that we can't. But failing to prioritize means that we will be perennially frustrated regardless of what we accomplish. For example, when Husband is out of town, my five priorities on any given weekday involve:

- getting Child to school;

- going to work;

- coming home early enough to take Child to extracurriculars;

- helping with homework; and

- working out.

Having a traditional (i.e., a media-portrayed) family dinner with actual main dish and side items just doesn't make the cut. I have a circulating library of reasons why a traditional sit-down dinner is not happening: (i) Husband is gone so there's no point in making anything complicated for two people; (ii) I'm tired; (iii) I didn't go to the store; (iv) I don't have the right tools; (v) I don't have time before getting Child to the next activity; (vi) we have to do homework; (vii) I just don't want to; and (viii) a minimalist charcuterie plate consisting of whatever slices of white cheddar and maybe a remnant of brie rind is sufficient and chic.

This is vastly different from my growing up experience, where my mother had nightly seated dinners for the entire family. But I would rather spend the mental energy with the other five priorities than worry about whether I'm a failure or setting Child up for a lifetime of delinquency. Luckily, my mother invites us over for a weekly Sunday night dinner, so Child is culturally exposed to what a traditional dinner is like. And I don't have to contribute anything that can't be bought from the store.

As discussed in "Reject the script" in Chapter V, it's ok if your "not everything is worth doing" includes not playing with your kids in the way they want.

Engaging with them doesn't have to be a unilateral decision. Children are like dogs. They will sense fear and discomfort through subliminal emotions and react accordingly. Half-heartedly engaging will just frustrate all parties—you will be distracted with thoughts of not wanting to do what you're doing, with the additional guilt of feeling like a horrible parent. And the child will respond with increasing desperation because they sense not all is well with the parent, but they can't intuit what it is and think that they have done something wrong to make the parent subliminally act this way.

Instead, just say no. Saying "no" to a child on their initial offer will not scar them for life; it will instead build resilience and help them learn the fine art of negotiation (see Chapter XI H.A.G.G.L.E). Then counter their initial offer by suggesting something that interests both of you. The sooner we can give ourselves permission to not be subjectively perfect, the sooner we can gain confidence in our choices.

Finally, to reiterate this point on cutting out the superfluous activities in our lives like we did with unnecessary baby items, let me tell you a story about Christmas a few years ago. The job I had at the time meant that I was extremely busy from October through December, the last quarter of both the calendar and my company's fiscal year. There was no opportunity to take two weeks off from the end of Child's school until after the New Year; work continued except for Christmas Eve and Christmas. Yes, even New Year's Day wasn't sacred.

I had this same job for two years up to this point—the end-of-year schedule was not a surprise. Yet despite that familiarity, I still succumbed to holiday pressures. Buying presents. Going to holiday parties. Making a signature dish for a dinner party. Desperate and frazzled at the end of every year, I vowed to change. *This year would be different. We're cutting back on presents. I won't go to a party if I don't want to. I will stay in control.*

In the third Christmas season with that job, December began in a fury and stayed manic. In the midst of my own work chaos, Husband's work kept him away frequently, which meant juggling primary caregiving activities and still volunteering at Child's classroom holiday party, because I am a masochist that at least recognizes classroom holiday party memories trump work responsibilities. At least for a few hours.

Husband's last stint kept him away from December 20-24. When he returned that night, he came home to find me alone, sitting on the floor of our bedroom in a bathrobe. All but one small nightstand light was turned off in the room. Present wrapping paraphernalia was strewn all about the floor. Just as he entered, I was attempting to muffle broken sobs to avoid Child overhearing them from his room next door. As I sat there, trying to wrap the pile of small gifts and avoid my tears wetting the paper, I knew it was over. I couldn't live like this. None of this was worth it. Somehow, I made it through that season, but the memory of that Christmas Eve stuck with me for the next ten months. Next time it would be different.

The following Christmas season was distinctly better. I still overcommitted myself. But I also made some solid progress in prioritizing my activities. After trying to fit in a family party hosted an hour's drive away and also committing to a dinner at my parents' house, I started to succumb to the pressure of holiday madness.

Once again, Child and I were flying solo.[19] The strict timeline I had set up to make this multi-step travel miracle happen started to unravel when we could not get out the door until thirty minutes past the deadline. Then five minutes into our trip I realized that I had forgotten the Christmas cards[20] that we were supposed to mail en route. We returned to the house for the cards and that's when I made the decision. Already under time pressure, I decided to forgo the family party. I don't know if my decision was negatively perceived by that side of the family. I never asked. After all, one should never ask a question one doesn't already know the answer to. But that decision

---

[19] Child and I were not actually flying, just at home. Husband was the only one that actually was flying solo in a plane full of other passengers. I am starting to recognize there is a pattern to his absences during holidays.

[20] This was the first Christmas in three years that we decided to expend the effort and make and send out Christmas cards. Technically, they are Christmas postcards because postcards have cheaper stamp rates.

saved my sanity that day[21] and helped me get through part of another holiday season. Things are looking optimistic this next year.

Delegation of tasks

Bonding with a child can take time. And bonding is hard to do if all we can think about are the unending list of actions that we need to accomplish and the limited time we have to complete them. We all know those mothers who for some reason or another assume the majority of child minding, diapering, watching, and engagement. Maybe they believe being a mother requires exclusive ownership of those things. Maybe they legitimately enjoy it. Maybe they have control issues. If you are one of those individuals, I marvel at your stamina. But for us mortals, delegating tasks to help us bond with accepting the stage of life we are in is key to survival.

---

[21] Since we didn't have to drive an extra hour, I was able to get to my parents' house early enough to help manage their Christmas dinner chaos. This earned a double-bonus of looking like I had my life together, at least for that half of my family.

Take a cue from Corporate America. No executive leader has risen to where they are by actually taking on more work. No, that's what the under-paids are for. The faster you can get a direct report, the faster you can start taking credit for their work in addition to yours. And what happens when you become that corporate super star? Why, you get promoted. And more underlings. And that glorious cycle continues until you find yourself a six-figure-with-stock-options sinecure. You know you've really made it when no one really knows what you do for your job other than attend meetings and delegate responsibility, but they are too afraid to ask.

If maternal stardom is what you crave, just delegate. No one really believes that you can have a serious career, volunteer at classroom parties, have a spotless house and stay in peak shape all by yourself without the help of childcare, corporate scheduling flexibility, cleaning help, and a will to look hot. As long as you don't post your secrets to the one platform all oversharing mommies frequent (Facebook), no one will ever know.

Husband's arrived from work and you've been stuck at home all day? Parental clock-in starts the second he walks in the door. Don't let feigned exclamations of tiredness (if he dares) sway you—being at home with something that is constantly clamoring for attention, trying to kill themselves, having to get changed, fed, or attended to is insurmountably more difficult. Believe me, I've been on both sides. Mondays were the best days at law school because I could recover after being home with Child all weekend. Sign me up for that corporate cubicle wasteland any day.

Delegation continues long after the early child years. At some point a parent will need to understand their limitations, particularly with homework. Child is (fortunately) gifted in math, which (unfortunately) means by the time he reaches 5th grade he will be beyond my capability of helping him. As such, Husband is the main arbitrator of math homework. If Husband is gone and help is needed, I utilize the Socratic method to enable Child's self-discovery of the answer while deflecting questions of my own inadequacy.

The over-scheduled mothers (myself included) in my community have mutual delegation down to a science. We constantly engage in a quid pro quo of carpool, gift pooling, and ad hoc hang outs. One would think that the constant pace would create an opportunity for abusing this goodwill. However, the societal pressures of living in an extremely small and gossip-prone community keep the incentives in favor of fairness.

Delegate, dear friends. Delegate like the idealized versions of your life depend on it. Because it does.

CHAPTER VII
S.E.L.F.

Motherhood doesn't take a holiday. What does one do with the problem of having fourteen waking hours in a day and needing to entertain a child for the majority of the time? Milk the hell out of that B. For fun-deprived, extroverted, or socially judged mothers like myself, a full calendar of activities really helped quiet the anxiety of feeling housebound by a baby-shaped ball and chain. Let's be real, having actual fun probably doesn't involve the small person that is now in your life. But in the interim, they can be part of some activities that *you* at least find fun.

But at this precarious time of life, even coming up with an agenda of fun can seem overwhelming. Don't let yourself get overwhelmed with trying to execute an internet post-worthy activity. Instead, utilize some S.E.L.F.-preservation: **S**hamelessly **E**mbrace **L**ow-hanging **F**ruit.

What I mean by "low-hanging fruit" is to first find the obvious or easy things to do with your child before moving on to more complicated ones. Creativity is like a muscle. The more one practices the easier it will be. Trying to come up with the "perfect" solution to fill the glut of daylight hours right off the bat is overwhelming. Why set yourself up for psychological failure?

Instead, take a note from my ancestors, who upon embarking on an arduous journey across the Appalachian Mountains and reaching the Midwest 150 years ago, decided that this flat and fruitful land was good enough. Now don't get me wrong, the Midwest does have a lot of perks, most of which reflect how much of an antisocial miscreant I really am. These good-natured people will forgive any driving transgression by not honking at the offender, even if the offender completely deserves it.

Midwesterners will actually converse with you on the street or in the grocery store. The basic standard of living is relatively affordable. There are opportunities to live in communities with decent public schools that do not require driving long distances or through ridiculous traffic. Aspiring for average has enabled millions of people to live, well, pretty good.

But just as a long journey starts with a single step, we must first put pen to paper and come up with actual ideas for S.E.L.F.-preservation. Because I've already graduated from actively filling Child's and my social calendars to now managing the never-ending onslaught of his school, friend, and extracurricular demands, I want to help you do the same. The three items below are easy ways to get started on your journey to reclaim S.E.L.F.

S.E.L.F.-preservation tip: Do what you find fun

If you have fun doing an activity, your child will too. This is a bit of a chicken and egg idea though, so bear with me. Being a creature of habit and not wanting to be bothered with creative thinking, one summer Child and I went to the zoo three to four times a week on average. Our record was five days due to exceptional boredom, but even that proved too much. Sure, the zoo was educational, but I went because I wanted to. To thwart the stroller brigade and multi-task an arm workout like the little try-hard that I was, I forwent a stroller and carried him Bonobo-style.

I loved the zoo for me: learning about different animals, appreciating the flora, and imagining what it would be like to make earrings out of the brightly colored beetle exoskeletons. But two hours of zoo time also meant that when we returned to our apartment, Child immediately went down for a long nap, so I earned two hours of responsibility-free time. In total, the math on a zoo day worked out in my favor—four hours of doing things that I enjoyed. It was glorious. And thanks to extensive zoo visits, now Child and I share lots of little inside jokes that only the most astute zoo enthusiasts would understand, like knowing exactly what I mean when I tell Child his hair looks like an East African Crowned Crane.

In addition to the zoo, up until the age of four, Child's primary external activities were (i) sitting in a stroller while I ran (ii) hitting a baseball off a tee in the backyard, (iii) going to any park, and (iv) finding the stuffed animal frog for a treat at the local Trader Joe's. He's turned out ok, even without Baby Mandarin classes or mommy-and-me yoga. The point is, everything is new and exciting to a child. Even things that are done frequently or routinely. Their short attention spans and poor perception of time means there will be sufficiently different factors to keep their interest and promote their growth as people. It doesn't have to be as hard as we make it.

Taking Child along with activities that interest me does have its limits, however. I recently attempted to bring Child to the mall. This was the result of a parade-of-horribles consisting of me wanting to go, no family available to watch him, my unwillingness to hire a babysitter, and Child being prohibited from going over to a friend's house due to grounding. My initial thought was taking Child to the mall meant he would be miserable and learn a lesson about making the poor choices which led to his grounding.

Unfortunately, this backfired on me spectacularly as I had absolutely zero fun while Child cloth-blocked me at every turn.

Do what you find fun but recognize it does have its limits. A three-hour boozy brunch may not be conducive to bringing along a child, but if you make the attempt, let me know how it turns out.

S.E.L.F.-preservation tip: Small things add up

Think about ways to incorporate small things that you already must do into something moderately amusing for your child as well. Then adapt them further to your child's unique interests. Now marvel at your genius.

If you have zero ideas on where to start and don't want to browse Pinterest because of the likelihood of a triggering moment from all of the perfectionistic mommy-types, just think of things that you liked to do as a child and repeat them. I promise you the children won't know.

Writing this book has enabled me to delve deeper into what my own mother faced with raising me, the firstborn. Most parents try their best, but let's face it, the firstborn is the experimental child. Apparently, I hated to have my shirt removed over my head before bath time or during diaper changes and would incessantly cry at every attempt. Knowing an alternate strategy was required, my mother began to shrewdly condition me to accept clothing changes by adopting the Pavlovian strategy. She created an original song, "T-shirt Head," which she would start to sing before the event began. Sure enough, "T-shirt Head" with the lyrics, "she's a T-shirt head," repeated for as long as it took to secure distraction, got the job done.

"T-shirt Head" was so successful, that it continued to evolve over the years. As firstborn, I adopted it to sing, "I'm a T-shirt head!" loudly and confidently as I pranced around my childhood bedroom with a T-shirt pulled halfway up my head and flipped inside out, obscuring my hair like a nun's habit. I also helped to proliferate her Pavlovian strategy with my younger siblings while they were getting their respective clothes changed. All of us were born with very large heads.

I later adopted the practice with Child, although I started much later, given that he was already conditioned to accept clothing changes due to my rougher handling. But he still enjoyed dancing around his room, nun's habit flapping with the movement, to "I'm a T-shirt head!"

Two other examples from Child's youth *that he still remembers and appreciates today* stand out as prime examples. Added bonus, they were completely free:

Example 1: Nap Notes. Child's preschool asked parents to write a nap note for their children that would be read to them at, you guessed it, nap time. At first, stress ensued when I knew I didn't have more than a week of variations of, "Have a great day, I love you!" Then I remembered the cliché, a picture is worth a thousand words. I then thought of how Child loved precious Puppy, who coincidentally looks like a rabbit. And thanks to an obsession with rabbits in elementary school, I could at least draw one that passably resembled. As such, I started drawing rabbit-dogs on his nap notes. Twenty seconds of effort and Child loved it. Rabbit-dog flying a plane, rabbit-dog with Child, rabbit-dog with a present. Soon I mastered Nap Note 2.0 when I started asking Child what scenario he would want to see. Child was happy for an opportunity to contribute to the creative process and I had one less item to think about. We all won.

Example 2: Coco About Town. Coco was a Boxer puppy stuffed animal that Child received as a gift from a neighbor when he was three. Coco became an immediate and special companion. Coco became even more important during Husband's second

deployment. Child's emotional state was slowly diminishing the longer the deployment dragged on and we both needed a little fun. Child couldn't bring Coco to school with him; because the loss of Coco would be absolutely devastating, Coco was not allowed out of the house unless it involved a carefully vetted overnight stay. However, we both thought it would be fun to have Coco visit me at work. Coco helped in a variety of capacities, such as answering phones, typing a memo, or reading over a brief. When Child came home from school, we would look at the pictures and laugh about how silly (Coco) and absurd (me) looked.

Whatever small things you choose to do, just make sure they don't become yet another dreaded obligation. These ideas are supposed to be fun and relatively effortless. Maybe your child, like mine, buys their lunch from school every day. Great! Don't stress that your small thing isn't writing a special note with an accompanying sticker on a napkin placed in a perfectly curated lunch box. Guess what, you have just preemptively saved your child in thirty years coming to grips with their own parenting limits and thinking that sending their own kid to school without a packed lunch meant that they have failed. Their future selves will now not develop a complex on yet another arbitrary action that is required of a devoted parent. You're a hero.

S.E.L.F.-preservation tip: Build in rest

We all know rest is critical. Adults need to incorporate rest into routines to allow time to think and process. Children also need downtime to use their imaginations, learn independence, and remember that their entertainment is not your sole mission in life.

The soonest children will understand how mentally and physically exhausting raising small things can be is when they will eventually have their own children. Unfortunately, your psyche can't wait that long, so your child will just need to understand that mother needs to get a break before she loses her shit. To that end, locking you and your child in a room together while you take a nap is a perfectly reasonable solution. My own mother recently reminded me that when I was a toddler, she would fall asleep (undoubtedly from pure exhaustion) while we were in my childhood bedroom playing. I would then entertain myself by opening my dresser drawers and trying on multiple outfits while piling the rejects onto the floor. After a while she would wake up, mostly refreshed, while I happily refined my keen personal style and reinforced the bad habits I still have as an adult in not putting my clothes away.

I adopted this strategy for the studio apartment that Child and I lived in during my 1L year. As I mentioned in "Boundaries to build relationships," I set up Child's Karlstad chaise-bed in the actual bedroom so that I could have a space to close the door to contain the chaos as needed. I likewise set up our TV and DVD player in his room so that I could utilize much needed screen time to distract Child while I passed out for a stress nap on the carpet. We were locked in the room together, Child blissfully playing away with his toys or mesmerized by Pixar, and I could have a brief worry-free respite. Those stress naps were sometimes the only things that enabled me to make it through one more day during that time.

Without a minimal amount of rest, life becomes quickly overwhelming and can cause everything to seem more upended than it really is. I know it sounds trite coming from someone who made it past that stage, but it doesn't make it less true. Do what you need to for both of you to make it through one more day. Even if it means leaving your child in a crib to go outside for a walk around the block, if that's the only thing keeping all mental hell from breaking loose. They will be there when you get back.

CHAPTER VIII
Living with
P.R.I.V.I.L.E.G.E.

Children should be reminded early and often of the privileges they have enjoyed. It's a little like a thankfulness journal where people write down things they appreciate in life, but it's done less gently.

Each of us has been gifted with privilege of some sort. Working at a military installation early in our marriage was the first time I realized that having an undergraduate degree was a privilege. Growing up, a college degree was a natural next step and not going to college would have been the anomaly. In contrast, a large segment of the surrounding population of the military installation did not have that opportunity and likely were not going to. My stay at the installation was temporary; I would use my degree to get better opportunities elsewhere. They could not. Having a college degree was a privilege; using that degree for upward mobility was yet another.

I must be transparent with the vast amount of privilege that I have in my life. Whether we realize it or not, the privilege that we experience is cumulative of the privileges derived from our parents, and their parents, and so on. Every generation provides an incremental gain. Some may be smaller than others, but at the very least they can teach the next generation lessons on what <u>not</u> to do in life. These negative lessons can be as valuable as the positive ones. The cumulative effect of this P.R.I.V.I.L.E.G.E. in our lives can be summarized as: **P**arental **R**esources **I**mparting **V**alue **I**n **L**ife, **E**njoyment, and **G**eneral **E**conomy.

I have privileges in the education I've received, privilege in my good health, privilege to have had an upbringing with a shockingly light amount of emotional baggage, privilege in the country that I've been born into—and much more. Child enjoys the privilege of inheriting his mother's hearty Midwestern stature, having parents deeply interested in his wellbeing and education, and having young grandparents who like to show him the finer things in life, like golf, that were never part of his own parents' education growing up.

Parental/Child privilege of "one and done"

Having one child reflects the privilege of the culture and country that we live in. I didn't have to be concerned that my country's child mortality rates meant there was a strong possibility Child wouldn't live to adulthood. I didn't need multiple children to secure the household livelihood. And when we decided that we would thwart convention and only have one child, Husband had the ability to get a vasectomy. I don't necessarily remember having a discussion that we would be "one and done," but apparently the feeling was instinctually mutual.

I got a most severe stink eye from a nurse when I filled out the questionnaire to give my consent for Husband's vasectomy. I don't necessarily blame the nurse. I may have written, "I DIDN'T WANT A CHILD" in capital letters. Bless that nurse, I was eight months pregnant and didn't give a *[insert very strong expletive here]*. Husband's snipping day became Child's original due date once I determined that I would forcibly evacuate Child early in order to avoid a forced military move with a one-week-old infant (thank you Tricare, love Dependa).

This privilege of Child being an Only is not just limited to him. As Child's parents, we derive a substantial amount of privilege from having a singleton. Having one child is the epitome of checking the box of Life. Sure, a kid completely destroys any semblance of pre-child life so things will never be the same, even when they grow up. But only having one child gives you responsibility street cred with other adults while making your life exceptionally less complicated. Sleepover at a friend's house? Turn that opportunity into an automatic date night and maybe a couple's workout at the gym the next morning. Need to run out for a trip to the store and don't feel like taking Child? Pinch-hitting a drop off favor for one is no issue.

Once we made the decision to be one and done, there was no looking back. Right or wrong, we knew we had to live with our decision. And honestly, we don't regret it at all. Thinking about *what ifs* expend needless energy. There's no such thing as an alternate timeline. As such, we've continued on and have adopted various strategies to mitigate the only-child effects as much as possible, like acting as Child's surrogate siblings ourselves by making him share his toys, taking turns, insisting on going first, and implementing merciless gaming strategies to win at any cost.

But this privilege of one and done isn't freely given. Privilege gets hers in return.

Having only one child comes with a lot of inherent risk, even outside of mortality. With one child, the theoretical child-rearing success rate could either be 100% or 0%. I am not a gambler but even I know those aren't good odds. Having more children can at least stretch the percentages to 50% or 66% if we're feeling optimistic and the numbers are in our favor.

Aside from Child's future theoretical success at being a productive member of society, another disadvantage of having an only child is that they will eventually shoulder the emotional burden of aging parents. Even excluding financial responsibility, Child will not have other siblings to reminisce about his childhood or pawn off alternating visitation schedules. He won't have a built-in support system of siblings, so he will need to establish one with his own immediate family and other friends.

All things considered, Child doesn't seem to be unduly harmed by his single-childness. Using a decade of acquired wisdom, Child firmly supports his singleton status. He doesn't have to share his toys and he has an enviable social life. In fact, he recently used being an only child as an example of his character strength for a school classroom activity.

Child may end up going the opposite direction of his parents and decide to have ten kids, but we fully support whatever he wants to do. After all, I'm not the one getting up in the middle of the night or changing diapers for twelve years.

Child privilege of resource concentration

While some parents may be forced to divide and conquer among multiple children, Child enjoys the privilege of our full attention on his personal and professional development.

I don't personally remember my own mother nagging me about homework. I think she may have started off asking me if I had any assignments and I was simply too honest to lie and say, "no." Looking back, this was decently effective. But this Mother knows improvements can be made. And she will build off that prior experience to enable Child to enjoy the P.R.I.V.I.L.E.G.E. of having dedicated homework enthusiasts.

Since I someday hope to lead a team of subordinates, I use Child as a trainee employee. At the start of every schoolyear, we measure short-term school grade expectations against the long-term goals of future academic and extracurricular pursuits. Goals are refreshed at the start of every semester, taking into account headwinds and feedback from previous months. As an added bonus to our weekly check-ins, he is also learning the fine art of corporate speak so that when he does encounter its use someday unironically, he will know when to wield them as either a shield to deflect suspicions of imposter syndrome or as a sword to belittle their absurdity.

With expectations presented, weekly check-ins gauge Child's current progress against those markers.

Reviewing grades has never been easier thanks to the ability to check overall grades and itemized assignments using online resources. Itemized assignment grading means Mother can pinpoint specific areas of weakness and use that data to concentrate on opportunities for precise development. Mondays are especially fun days because many of these online resources have an automatic email function so you don't have to spend needless time and corporal energy logging on manually. Instead, your child's grade report will be waiting patiently for you in your inbox when you wake up. Afraid of the eventual AI revolution? You don't have to be, as long as they're conditioned to being delegated your dirty work.

Information in hand, I can now use periodic touchpoints to raise key questions to Child such as:

"How are you doing?"[22]

and

"Do you have all of the resources that you need to get your job done?"

Sometimes the conversation will shift into his current extracurriculars, as will the inevitable question of what he wants to be when he grows up. Undoubtedly Child will offer up wanting to be an MLB[23] player and we'll go from there:

"Ok, that's nice, what is your fallback?"

and

"What are you doing now to get you closer to that goal rather than farther away?"

As the weeks fly by, the steady drumbeat of academics and extracurriculars accelerates into a feverish reprioritization of activities to meet quarter-end goals. Extracurriculars become a bargaining chip between

---

[22] By asking this question armed with data, you know exactly what the answer should be before it's asked. Well done.

[23] Major League Baseball, in case anyone is too embarrassed to ask or never played ball sports.

Mother and Child and fall quickly down the priority list if baseline numbers aren't on track. End of quarter activity is in full force as Child attempts to beat his grade percentages into submission.

Ultimately, my goal in pushing him is so that he will become far more successful than me. That being said, this Mother doesn't love Child enough to pay thousands of dollars on illicit college admissions. One must draw the line somewhere. One thing is for certain, an education is useless without understanding how to apply it.

By the time he was five years old, it was obvious Child appreciated money. Now, depending on the day, he wants to be a combination of either a coder or an investment banker or a baseball player. Ever observant of Child's gifts and interests, Mother agrees his care and appreciation for money likely makes him a great candidate for the former. After receiving a coin counter for Christmas last year, Child went immediately to work hustling relatives for the opportunity to count loose change for a 1% fee. He also seemed to have an inherent understanding of the value of money. He has never been one to make poor trading decisions at school, like paying $5 for a piece of candy. We've had to instead make sure he traded ethically with his less intuitive peers and not become the schoolyard usurer.

Regardless of that potential, we are still from and remain in the most unassuming area in the U.S. (aside from those times when every four years we are deemed politically important). Child living in the logical opposite of a banking mecca does put a bit of a damper on this hypothetical future career. But while the Midwest is not exactly a bastion of financial career opportunities, there's plenty of time to contemplate a family move or at least try to cater enough influence to go elsewhere. And why wouldn't we? He's an only child.

Child privilege of toy purchases

Child's privilege extends further to a certain flexibility on parental willingness to purchase toys. To Child's credit he's never been into single-purpose plastic toys. This is probably due in large part to Husband and I having "cut the cable cord" before Child's birth and Netflix hasn't introduced commercials (yet). As such, Child was never exposed to traditional TV and those heinous toy commercials, so he really doesn't know better. Most of his treasured possessions have been sports gear, stuffed animals, or the Simpsons Clue board game my parents gave to me in college.

Growing up in a closely observed neighborhood allows Child to benefit from playing with his friends' toys routinely while they run from house to house. Moreover, while Child and his friends enjoy a what's-mine-is-yours situation funded by their respective parents, the parents benefit with an if - the - toy - somehow - ends - up - at - your - house - please - do - me - a - favor - and - just - keep - it - so - I - have - one - less - object - cluttering - my - very - small - but - very - expensive - house - because - of - steadily - rising - property - taxes - and - pre-bubble - (again) - housing - affordability - crisis understanding.

A downside of living within such close neighborly quarters means one well-meaning parent can unwittingly set off an arms race of toy acquisition. In

Child's case, three different boys within a three-block radius received dirt bikes for their birthdays. Child was enthralled with the idea of the dirt bike bringing an adrenalin fix and freedom of movement. Husband and I wanted to live vicariously through Child because we would have relished the independence and general bad-assedry when we were his age. We ultimately gave Child the option to get a dirt bike for his birthday on the stipulation that a dirt bike would be his only gift (it's not cheap) and his birthday party would otherwise be very low-key. He chose the dirt bike. Now, normally Child chooses to have a fun birthday party over presents, which Mother thoroughly approves. However, in this instance Child logically took the long-term view of comparing a birthday party experience by X minutes of joyriding over the lifespan of the bike and came out miles ahead of a two-hour party. Luckily for other neighborhood parents, Child has been very generous with his dirt bike and further escalation has been avoided.

Parental privilege of giving back earlier

Being one and done allows us to pass on the privilege of finding more time for non-child activities sooner than multi-child peers. We all know how mentally and physically difficult raising young children can be. As they grow older and become more self-sufficient, this same energy can be channeled into different activities, like volunteering in the community, engaging in activities that you find personally enjoyable, or being able to take the time to pursue on-hold life goals.

Trying to get a mental or physical break when having small children can feel like dog-paddling in quicksand. Any encouragement, no matter how small, can be the buoy to bring us through one more day. When Child was two years old, I attended a bridal shower at the tail end of my 1L year and Husband's first deployment. Morale was low. But I had the opportunity to catch up with a family friend—a kind and beautiful matriarch who is the type of person one would hope to be at that stage of life. As I began to overshare the amount of stress I felt, she listened and didn't try to respond with any trite mommy-ism of,

"You'll miss it when he's older" or "But this is the best job in the world!" She instead simply acknowledged the situation and assured me that it's ok to not feel like others do about motherhood or this stage of life. It may have seemed inconsequential. But it meant a lot in that moment.

I've tried to do the same with other struggling moms I see, although I probably don't think about it as much as I should. Five years after the bridal shower, Child and I were enjoying ourselves at a pool, just the two of us. The sky was a vibrant blue, a light breeze rustled the palm trees and you could hear the faint sound of the waves breaking against the beach in the background. Best of all? Child was playing in the pool with some new friends he had made. While I still kept a soft eye on him, I could avoid actually having to be in the pool and get a bit of a break.

I noticed another young mother who was obviously struggling to not get (understandably) frustrated with managing two young children at the pool. The youngest, an immobile baby, stayed locked to her hip while she managed an eager three-year-old who wanted to play in the shallow end of the pool. As I watched her interact with her children, I sensed her getting increasingly frustrated. Maybe she was frustrated with feeling tired. Or that she felt like she wasn't doing enough to play with the older one. Or that she was having to attempt a pool visit without family to help. Maybe she was just trying to keep her sanity until naptime. I felt like I had to tell her that she was doing a great job and she was a great mom. So, I did. Her tired eyes smiled back, and then hesitantly said, "Thank you, I don't feel like it sometimes." That was the extent of our interaction. She left shortly after, towing both children back (I assume) to her room for a snack and a nap. I continued to watch Child in the pool until he likewise got hungry and wanted to leave.

It was not until writing this book that I realized I should have stepped outside of my comfort zone and offered to help. Maybe that could have meant even more to that tired mom than mere words. But I didn't think to do it at the time because I was tired too, even if not to the extent that she was. As we veteran mothers start to age into different life stages, we have an opportunity. We can fill the space vacated by that maturing child and support other women in their stages. We can offer encouragement. Or volunteer to watch their children so that they can get away by themselves. And finally, we can offer empathy.

I fully recognize the privilege that I have in this stage of life. And now I can exploit that privilege for the good of humanity. Having the capacity to even think about consistently devoting the time to volunteer activities can be a slow road. And that's ok, you may not yet have the opportunity to Delegate (see Chapter VI B.O.N.D.) some of your activities to others to get there faster.

Although volunteerism is noble, it doesn't mean it can't be fun or feel easy. Reflect back to Chapter VII S.E.L.F. and shamelessly exploit the low-hanging fruit that are your own personal interests. Whatever you do, don't try to do something you're not passionate about. The lack of interest will be apparent to everyone and then you'll just resent having given up several precious hours of your personal time. And try to not let the pull of volunteering at a work event get too overwhelming. Why volunteer to lead an event with your professional organization if the last thing you want to do is put on a show in front of certain colleagues you otherwise want to avoid? Save the leadership for organizations and people that you truly care about and that deserve your input. And if you really need the work credit, then circulate an internal article to your colleagues describing the event after-the-fact, along with strategically photographed pictures to enhance attendee numbers and relative impact.

Privilege of making your own choices

It's easy to take the privileges we have for granted, particularly if we tend to focus on ourselves rather than observe those around us. By engaging with others, we gain the benefits of appreciating the privileges we enjoy, with added empathy for others' experience.

Making a choice to pursue a different or unfamiliar path isn't easy. I had trouble in the early years of motherhood reconciling my path from that of my mother's. My mother is very smart. But when she was growing up very few women were encouraged to pursue medical school. And even fewer did. She could have been a doctor, had that been something she would have been encouraged to be and she felt supported in pursuing. Given the cultural restraints, she became a nurse. Once she became pregnant with me, she stopped working. (Yes, I was the doc-block.) She then had four more children. She is happy, feels fulfilled, and loves her children and grandchildren. But I struggled with the lack of choice she had with her potential career and the cultural expectations of her life. I felt angry and sorry that she did not have the opportunities that I enjoyed. While we had many similarities, our paths were irreparably divergent.

Yet I was the one who misjudged her. While working as a nurse, she had the choice to pursue being a doctor. But then she found out that she was pregnant. And she chose to not become a doctor and instead, stay home to have children. I faced the same circumstance and chose to still pursue a career after having a child.

We both faced career choices. We chose differently. Neither of us regrets our choice; both of us respect the other for it. And that is the ultimate manifestation of privilege.

CHAPTER IX
P.A.T.T.E.R.N.

Patterns are rife within nature. Patterns are comforting. Familiar. They enable us to live on autopilot and not expend needless brainpower. They calm our minds, when otherwise we would race from one stimulus to the next in our driven and overly scheduled society. Humans fall into patterned behavior because we are perpetually lazy creatures. Patterns touch every aspect of our lives and every subject we study. And if we stop to actually think and begin to observe them, one can readily see the patterns that we (and others) engage in.

My first memory of studying patterned behavior happened in high school with a very tough history teacher. I was a majority A student, so I was perfectly capable of doing well. But my hubris was short-lived. We took the first test one month into the quarter and I scored an abysmal 77%. This was not acceptable. History and English were my core strengths.

Determined to do better, I began reviewing what went wrong. In studying the exam and class notes, I recognized two key items: (i) any lists written on the classroom whiteboard would be on the test; and (ii) anything underlined on that same board would most certainly be essay questions on the test. Once I made those connections, I studied the corresponding material and scored a 99% on her next exam.

Without knowing it at the time, I had reduced pattern observation into two distinct areas: **Step 1**: Find or create patterns of behavior through observation. **Step 2**: Harness the pattern and exploit it for personal gain. Coincidentally, these two steps can be succinctly summarized as:

Planned

Attention

To

Track and

Exploit

Routines and

Needs

Child is now being taught the fine art of pattern-seeking in his own schooling.

Every school year proves new challenges, and this year is no different. One of Child's elementary school teachers, who we will call Mrs. J, runs on patterns of teaching that are older than I am. Mrs. J is less than five years away from retirement so freshening up her teaching style is not a good ROI for her at this point. Child legitimately likes Mrs. J as a person. But her class is relatively difficult, especially for Child who unfortunately does not appreciate the fine nuances within language arts. She's also the only teacher who submits grades within the tenth of the decimal, which

I respect. Mrs. J isn't shy about doling out assignments, which, from a percentage standpoint, creates lots of opportunities to make As. But too many low grades also make a comeback statistically impossible.

Fourth grade means Child needs to own his homework and communicate with his teachers. This is not my decision—it was prescribed in parent handouts given at the beginning of the year precisely to reel in over-involved individuals like myself. And yes, I've obeyed. I always follow directions. But as hard as it has been to let go, that doesn't mean that I can't transition into providing guidance based on observations.

Several academic weeks and a back-to-school event provided enough recon where Mother very closely observed patterns of grading and resource instruction to determine the P.A.T.T.E.R.N. strategy.

Step 1: **Find or create patterns of behavior through observation**. In this case, Mrs. J provided handouts to the parents that referenced not only the weekly loose-leaf worksheets she gave to the students but also a workbook. Her routine quizzes indicated that she paid special attention to the irregular examples of parts of speech and examples of synonyms/antonyms for vocabulary.

Step 2: Harness the pattern and exploit it for personal gain. Armed with new information, Mother incorporated the quizzes and workbook into Child's daily study review. Those things, coupled with increased supervision for diligent study, resulted in many more As. It's still a hard-fought struggle for Child to make above a 90% on most language arts assignments, but Child is well on his way to using this as one of many examples of hard work and an excruciatingly interested parent to overcome his many first world problems.

For those parents who are just beginning their child-rearing journey, I will now give you the two greatest examples of pattern detection and exploitation that you never knew you needed. Each example demonstrates how a P.A.T.T.E.R.N. can be used to (i) build a habit and (ii) break a habit.

Example 1: Sleep minimalism (build a habit)

Most parents will have at least one area in which they take exceptional pride in during their child-rearing experiences. Some parents may have only feeding their child organics. Others may have no screen time. My magnum opus is sleep training. The foundational question to my start on the sleep training attempt was of course, *what is the easiest for me?* The answer to that being, minimize effort at bedtime and train Child to be the most low-maintenance and easiest sleeper imaginable.

In order to sleep train Child, I first had to do what any good plane rider is taught and put my own oxygen mask on first before attempting to help the weak. Now, I am an unusually light sleeper to begin with. I have not independently confirmed, but I maintain the firm belief that being a firstborn meant I was permitted to sleep in absolute silence. This has historically crippled me to the point where I must wear earplugs at night, even if my foghorn blowing Husband is not home. I vowed I would do better for Child. After he was born, Child spent exactly three days sleeping in the same room as me. The first two were at the hospital. The last was the first night at home. He hiccupped and moved so much in his crib I couldn't sleep. And if Mother can't sleep then no one will.

I moved Child to his room (the converted office with a temporarily erected playard) down the short hallway from mine. I could hear just as well without aid so I forewent yet another object that could scream at me (the baby monitor) and just left our door open. I slept much better. Aside from the waking every few hours to feed.

The first bit of advice several parenting experts dictated to me was in order to put the child down to sleep, one must have a routine. A calming, gentle routine for both mother and baby. First, the nighttime routine would commonly begin an hour before sleep. The gentle mother will cycle her way through bathing the child, applying full body lotion, fresh diapering, and if the mother truly loves her child, a gentle infant massage. Then the baby must be encased in a full swaddling blanket and transported to the nursery.

Loving mother will balance her baby burrito in one arm as she carefully dims the room lights to the level where activities can still be done but it's dark enough that the child will intuit bedtime. The fresh diaper just placed will be quickly replaced as the child should be offered another chance to feed before being placed in the crib. Post-feeding, the child should be rocked and snuggled for at least another fifteen minutes and maybe include a song and selected book reading. This is the penultimate bonding experience. It is serene. Transcendent. It evokes the purity of a mother-child relationship. It was not for me.

The fatal flaw I quickly discovered was that a routine would actually have to be established and consistent in order to follow it. This was in fact inapposite to what I wanted to do. I didn't want to create a slave to subjective conditioning. I needed a kid who could face uncertainty and decide that instead of being disrupted he would go to sleep. I chose the nuclear option.

When I deemed it to be Child's bed time (as early as possible to give me at least a two hour buffer before I likewise went down)…

…I placed him in his crib while he was still awake. That's it. No books. No rocking. No bath. No lavender-scented baby lotion that supposedly helped children fall asleep but would not somehow trigger a dermatological reaction on virgin skin. The beauty of this regimen is *if the routine was only placing Child in bed, it could never get broken.* Child managed this spectacularly. I may have potentially blocked this out of my memory, another trait inherited from my mother, but I don't recall excessive crying in reaction to this routine, particularly since I recall so many other latent traumas from that time. It's been ten years, and Child is still brilliantly flexible with bedtime routines and is frequently invited to sleepovers as a neutral and easy-going playmate.

In full disclosure, Child was an early adopter of thumb-sucking, which helped with his sleep habits. I welcomed the opportunity to not get woken up by a frantic infant who could not locate a pacifier in the dead of night, so I did nothing to stop him. With a thumb attached to his body, he could quickly fall back to sleep. This habit continued for several years until we decided to break it (see Example 2 below).

An unintentional but happy accident discovered during sleep training was that while Child was sleep training and spending his first year and a half alive, we lived in an apartment complex brimming with hipsters. And these hipsters were not like us. No, while we were twenty-six, married and saddled with a baby, they did not waste a minute of a Saturday night. So, Child learned to sleep to the methodic beat of weekend parties. Coincidentally or not, he is a big fan of music now.

Those early patterns of behavior have indeed served Child well. He still can fall dead asleep within ten minutes of lying down. With our bedrooms right next to each other, it's a useful skill to help ward off opportunities of embarrassment from overhearing late-night activities.

Example 2: Blankie ban (break a habit)

Child received no less than six blankets as gifts before he was born. Although competition was fierce, Child ended up imprinting on a satin-lined blue and white blanket around the time he was one. "Blankie" was meticulously watched and loved by all. Mother would stop at nothing to make sure Blankie was not left anywhere accidently and, like Coco, his presence outside of the house was strictly controlled. There was only one unfortunate incident where Blankie was left at daycare overnight and it was never repeated.

Child kept Blankie by his side until he was three years old. Conventional wisdom dictates that children should be weaned from thumb sucking around that time in order to avoid dental issues once their adult teeth start to emerge. Whether or not this recommendation is still accurate ten years later, I committed to it at the time for two reasons: (i) I wanted to minimize the potential for misaligned teeth or speech issues in order to save money on future remediation, and (ii) after age three, parents should help their children develop better coping mechanisms.

A quick search of the 2020 trash vacuum reveals that suggested techniques to overcome thumb sucking are (and I am not exaggerating): (i) gently asking them; (ii) offering tea; (iii) having someone else tell them to stop because they won't listen to you (how is that for a wakeup call on the effectiveness of your parenting?); (iv) bitter nail polish; and (v) a $40 plastic or fabric thumb guard bandage so that when worn, the child sucks on an unappetizing medium rather than supple skin and is incentivized to quit.

First, mad respect for any parent who can put a thumb guard on a child's hand and keep them actually wearing it. Trying that technique on Child would have landed us both in serious therapy. Instead, I decided on good old-fashioned manipulation. I began by observing Child's thumb sucking patterns. After several days of close observation, I determined that Child had a ritual where at bedtime he would grasp his blanket with his right hand while lying down and begin to repetitively rub the satin edge among his right thumb, index and pointer fingers. This motion in play, he would settle back, insert his left thumb into his mouth and head off to dreamland.

I surmised that by taking away the trigger blanket, and substituting with an equally loved plush toy, the thumb sucking habit would be disrupted. Hypothesis constructed; the experiment began. Blankie was respectfully removed, folded into a somber triangle and placed discreetly in a drawer. Coco the Boxer puppy was used as the substitute comfort toy. Now to observe. Child gratefully cuddled with his sweet Coco but that's as far as it went. No smooth satin trigger meant Child stopped sucking his thumb almost immediately. No thumb sucking observed, hypothesis confirmed. We waited about six months before reintroducing Blankie back into the fold in order to maintain a suck-free environment. Child did not relapse.

I'm not going to claim this approach to solving the issues of sleep training or thumb sucking will work for everyone. These approaches worked in our use case for a number of reasons: (i) Starting early; (ii) not putting up with bullshit, and finally, (iii) Child's relatively easy-going personality (refer back to (ii)). Observing and exploiting relevant patterns will not always be such a quick and easy process. It may take time to reach a satisfying outcome. And that's ok. As we ladies have experienced too often, finishing fast is not always the best.

CHAPTER X
Be R.E.A.L.

After watching Child's baseball team get absolutely destroyed by a far superior team, I thought creating an appropriate life lesson from the ruins of chaos would be the best way to recover lost personal dignity. Because that's exactly what normal mothers do.

I hate failure. Even past disappointments that shouldn't bother me anymore still tend to sting if I dwell on them too much. One large failure I still try to move beyond is my failed tween acting career. In addition to excessive vanity, another outcome of my prolific childhood Barbie playing was a desire to become an actress. To accomplish this goal, I embarked on a season of weekly acting classes and annual school play auditions. You rightly guess that because I am talking about this experience within the context of failures that I was unsuccessful.

As disappointments mounted during middle school, that dream faded away. That is, until my senior year of high school. Yes, I finally made it by successfully auditioning for the musical *Godspell* and being cast in the role of the Sexy Disciple, one of the main supporting characters. Now at that time, I was a quiet girl with pale skin and mouse brown hair. This was the exact opposite of the coveted tan skin and sun kissed highlights for any high school female in the early aughts. I was certainly not sexy. So how in all possible roles was this the one to bring me out of my eight-year dry spell? Well, what I didn't tell you was that at the time I went to a Christian school. And I surmise that the decision to cast me as the Sexy Disciple was not due to my raw talent, but because I could do an adequate job without making the character actually sexy for the audience.

Before imaginations run wild and anyone starts extrapolating this experience to the other classic early-aughts movie stereotypes of the high school cinematic dramady, let me stop you right there. This cute but quiet, odd girl did not then suddenly turn hot and get the popular guy. My life afterward was still underwhelmingly average. In reality, my awkwardness continued and it was still another three years before I had my first (and only) real boyfriend.

We all have examples of things we've tried, and failed, and continued to fail at despite unyielding persistence. Failure is inevitable. But failure isn't the end. When disappointed with a failure, we need to be R.E.A.L.:

Reflect on what happened

Evaluate what can be improved

Act to correct

Look over results and adjust as needed

Applying R.E.A.L. to real life

We inadvertently go over the steps to **Reflect**, **Evaluate**, **Act**, and **Look** in small ways every day. Whether it's determining that multiple bowls of ice cream just before bedtime leads to poor quality sleep and feeling bloated in the morning, or that the false set of eyelashes we decided to self-apply to save money were done a little too hastily so they appear slightly cock-eyed, questioning whether the it was worth the savings. There's a myriad of opportunities to tap into further improvement.

Failure is painful. But failure is an opportunity to grow. Multiple outcomes emerge when applying the R.E.A.L. strategy in real life. Sometimes we use the lessons learned from the initial failure to try again to get a better outcome. Other times we may need to realize that in our eagerness to succeed, we're falling prey to the Sunk Cost Fallacy[24] and just need to stop completely. Or a third possibility is that we end up taking a hybrid approach; quitting temporarily and then restarting once circumstances change.

Let me be real with you and let you in on a little secret. In no time in my personal history have I been a competent cook. And I've never been able to mask that incompetency. It's actually one of three reasons why I decided to pursue a career, the second being not wanting to be a stay-at-home mom. I'll remain reticent on the third reason for now.

---

[24] The "Sunk Cost Fallacy" means that rather than quit an activity that is turning out to be too expensive, a bad idea, or otherwise unsuccessful, there is a strong tendency to continue with such activity due to the amount of time, money and energy that has already been invested in it and can't be recovered. Cambridge Business English Dictionary. Copyright Cambridge University Press. https://dictionary.cambridge.org/us/dictionary/english/ sunk-cost-fallacy. Accessed July 25, 2020.

As a newlywed, I made all sorts of meals that I still cringingly remember twelve years later. Frozen salmon cooked medium-rare doesn't quite have the same special quality as fresh, but I tried. Avocado "guacamole" crafted with lower-fat avocado abominations that thankfully don't exist anymore is something no one should experience. Shriveled oven-baked chicken that must have come from a pre-pubescent hen because they certainly didn't resemble any breasts that I've ever seen. And an enticing meal that I adapted from a legitimate recipe my mother in-law-gave me, but I consistently didn't have the right ingredients for, which I lovingly called: Garbage Dump Enchiladas.

So why, as a new mother, would I attempt to make baby food and believe this occasion would be any different? Because oxytocin makes you think things are better than they really are. That's their sole purpose and they won. Bastards.

Now, clever reader, you may look at this situation and rightly assume that making baby food isn't hard. At its simplest it is mashed or pureed fruits and vegetables. Even monkeys make that. Well yes, you are correct. But we are not monkeys. We are people and have advanced farther than that. When I read the "am-AY-zing" trash vacuum articles about doctoring your baby's food and creating a sophisticated baby pallet by adding additional herbs and spices, I immediately bought into the hype.

If I had been able to read W.I.S.D.OM. at the time, I may have realized that baby pallets are adaptable and I didn't need to push myself so far out of my comfort zone. I also may have felt more secure in my own abilities and didn't think I needed to prove my mother-ish ways by going 110% to the effort. But I didn't. Instead, I tried to conceal my inability and attempt the impossible. The garlic powder I put in Child's smashed pea lunch upset his stomach until he vomited garlic-laced green over both of us. The cinnamon I sprinkled on his sweet potato puree burned his sensitive lips until they were red with irritation. Thankfully, I had enough sense to stop right there, thanks to being R.E.A.L. with myself.

I **reflected** on the fact I was a shit cook.

I **evaluated** whether or not this was something I wanted to devote energy to. (No.) As such, I determined that was the last time I would doctor Child's food.

I **acted** to just buy pre-made like the heathen that I am.

Looking over results, it was determined that Child thrived on store-bought just fine.

I continued with my low-bar food preparation for more than nine years. When Child turned ten years old, I finally decided that it's time to not live like we're in college. Don't get me wrong, unless someone else is making a main with sides, a fresh pot of Kraft, spaghetti or hot dogs are still staples. But at least we're breaking out the dried sage every now and then. I am awaiting the day Child asks why we never had the conventional dinners that are portrayed on TV, at which point we will have a nice discussion on false imaging in the media and sexist stereotypes.

Now here's an exciting conclusion to this food story. Once Child reached nearly double digits, I had a little more breathing room to prioritize self-improvement.

I began to **reflect** on whether it's time to try this cooking thing again.

I **evaluated** school and work schedules to determine workweek feasibility and whether it was worth it to buy a cookbook (why buy the cow when the milk's free on the internet?). But then I found a cookbook for driven runners who want to be as efficient in the kitchen as they are in their workouts and I thought that even if I failed, I would have at least done my part to support two amazing female entrepreneurs.

I **acted** to purchase the ingredients and make the attempt. And after making turkey meatballs without screwing it up, Husband was legitimately impressed.

Looking over results, he was so impressed that now he shops and cooks for the meals using this same cookbook as long as I let him know what recipe sounds good and he's in town to take care of it. I have great aspirations of what culinary adventures we can conquer for our next ten years with my Husband's efforts at the kitchen helm, and my support behind him.

Teaching Child to be R.E.A.L.

Given the elementary school Child and his friends attend is not exactly a bastion of athleticism, they certainly have many opportunities to practice experiencing failure. And with that failure, they have several options on how to respond. They can feel utterly defeated and never try again. They can whine and blame the other team or the ref's bad calls and go back to their normal life. Or they can try to improve.

A thorough probing of a failed venture is not a common practice, regardless of age. Unbiased self-reflection is even more difficult; rarely do we believe ourselves to be the one at fault in a situation and instead blame external factors. What's more, the older we get, the more stuck in our ways we tend to remain. But unbiased and persistent reflection is a critical factor in our personal development. Particularly for those who are already gifted with enormous self-confidence, such as the only child of two firstborns.

No one likes to replay a situation that up until that point may have been the biggest example of failure or disappointment that they had in life. Especially when tender emotions are so raw. To begin **reflecting** on a failure (usually related to sports), Mother and Child begin with a light *voir dire*. Questions begin generally:

"How do you feel?"

"Did you have fun?"

and descend to more specific topics:

"If you could change one thing you did, what would it be?"

"What happened during that play?"

The tone is kept lighthearted and intent on learning. Then reflection evolves to personal **evaluation**. Is there a specific skill that Child should practice between now and the next game? Does Child need to have a more teachable attitude? Does Mother need to calm the F down and make sure she's not inadvertently causing Child unnecessary anxiety about his performance?

We all know change won't happen without personal buy-in. As such, it's critical that any evaluation resulting action come from Child himself. If this ultimately proves impractical, Mother will advise Child on what this should be, but follow through is going to be a lot more difficult and less effective.

After evaluating performance to find an area that can be improved, Child is encouraged to take **action**. Child can be self-driven, particularly if he is bored. But carrots and sticks may also be needed. Parental intervention may mean encouraging Child to practice (practice starts to look really enticing compared to doing chores) or withholding screen time. **Looking over results** to see if adjustments need to be made is the most challenging step because it takes a parent to lead the evaluation. And with all of the other priorities parents constantly must rotate, it may not be worth continuing to engage with an activity that was just pushed aside for more pressing matters.

While I was developing this R.E.A.L. approach in the car ride back from that fateful baseball game at the beginning of this chapter, I was expecting to mediate a whining session on the thirty-minute drive home. What actually happened was Child quickly got over any disappointment he felt and instead started talking about aliens and Area 51. The lesson for me on this one was I tend to overthink (a lot) and instead just need to **Reflect**, **Evaluate**, **Act**, and **Look** at myself and my expectations with Child. Not everything is a critical teaching moment.

CHAPTER XI

H.A.G.G.L.E.

Do I want Child to challenge me? No. Do I want him to challenge a future boss or colleague? Abso-freaking-lutely. Ergo, I die to my present desire of an easy, compliant child to demonstrate an overarching principle intended to further Child's success.

Women have traditionally failed to negotiate. It's a stereotype and I hate it. Unfortunately, I made this mistake after not countering the initial offer at my first job out of law school. Negotiating for a higher salary was not even on my mind at that time due to (i) my previous jobs being for hourly wages and not realizing those could also be negotiated; (ii) not understanding the value I bring to the organization;[25] and (iii) let's face it, the sheer fact that I was just happy to get a job during a tough economy. A year into the role, I realized that I should have countered, so I started to campaign for a raise. My advocacy continued for over a year, but unfortunately, nothing changed. In the interim, after realizing that negotiations were not going anywhere, I started looking for a different job. Once I got an offer for the new job, I knew I wouldn't make the same mistake again.

The art of H.A.G.G.L.E

The approach to how I parent would be 99%[26] the same, regardless of Child's sex. And as a parent, I know sooner or later, every person will encounter situations that require them to negotiate, or *haggle*, for a better outcome in life. Knowing how and when to

---

[25] Honestly, this comment is debatable because new attorneys really don't know anything and must be trained, but the key thing is that we convince others we do and then actually show it before suspicions set in.

[26] Unabashed disclosure here: Raising a girl would absolutely require a larger clothing budget as to me it's essentially dressing a real-life Barbie.

negotiate is critical to master. And negotiating effectively is a learned skill. Whether or not Child will end up in law, business, or really any other field, it's never too early to learn the art of preempting answers to anticipated questions. The sooner children can get started, the better.

To effectively H.A.G.G.L.E., Child must first organize his thoughts. Organization will enable him to review potential arguments, reasons to support his position, and answers to anticipated questions. Through this exercise, he can maximize his chances of a successful outcome. As such, Child very early on has been refining the art of the H.A.G.G.L.E.:

Humility

Acknowledge failure or limitations

Give examples of how to improve

Go-getter attitude

Lay out timeline

Evoke empathy

H.A.G.G.L.E. for reduced punishment

Teaching Child how to H.A.G.G.L.E. was originally birthed out of responding to a disciplinary incident, but the beauty of H.A.G.G.L.E. is that it can be used for so much more.

A bad choice and the ensuing disciplinary actions are highly subjective. A myriad of factors, such as incident, age, resulting injury, general attitude, patterns of behavior, mitigating circumstances, and many more, can go into a parent's decision in how to respond to a negative incident. While sometimes these sanctions are punitive, other times they are used as a negotiation opportunity to allow Child to plead his case for a reduced sentence. Therefore, he can H.A.G.G.L.E. for reduced punishment.

If Child makes a choice that requires discipline, Child will need to learn that when he is in the wrong, he must take responsibility and work to set things right for both himself and the injured party. The first step in how to H.A.G.G.L.E. for reduced punishment is to approach it with an air of **humility**. Child is indeed negotiating as the weaker party in every way. Showing humility from the start is a way to immediately build rapport with the parent for a successful outcome. Tone and perspective can make or break an opportunity to successfully negotiate a reduced punishment.

Ancillary to humility, **acknowledging failure** from the start of the negotiation assures the unhappy Mother that Child is aware an infraction was committed and that he recognizes the seriousness of the matter. Child can then **give examples** of what he can do to avoid causing the same issue in the future. Examples must be concrete and not abstract. For example, if the infraction involved ignoring parents' requests to get off Xbox at a certain time to do other activities, an example of, "I'll try harder" doesn't quite convey the same understanding as, "I will set an alarm to for the time I have to get off Xbox." Giving examples that directly link the action that led to this disciplinary intervention and what can be done to avoid it in the future shows he gets it. And it shows that he has measured ways to improve future performance. This improvement element is the pinnacle of those efforts. Pass this, and the momentum will carry Child through the rest of the chain to the end of a successful negotiation.

While some of our colleagues may be able to get away with being an *idea man* without actually taking action, I'm not training Child to be middle management. Which is why Child will demonstrate that not only can he creatively solve the problem, but he can see it through to a positive conclusion with a **go-getter attitude**. Following this, Child will **lay out a timeline** to implement the examples he gave two steps prior. Parental intervention may be needed to help Child form a realistic timeline for the identified solution.

During the H.A.G.G.L.E. process, Child has been methodically building his case for a more favorable outcome. The final step is to channel Aristotle and bring out the pathos. For while Mother may be a stone-cold sphynx and immune to common emotional pleas, Mother is powerless against the tight use of rhetoric. To complete this negotiation sandwich, **evoke empathy** by reminding Mother that she too was a child once and (try as she might) still makes mistakes. And, like, respectfully Ma, Child is only ten and this isn't ancient Greece.

H.A.G.G.L.E. for chores

Learning how to H.A.G.G.L.E. quickly expanded from disciplinary matters to negotiating some sweet coin for chores. Unbeknownst to me, Child made the mistake early on to accept the first offer Husband gave him for a job. As such, Mother had to step in and prep Child for the next opportunity to reopen negotiations.

When countering a low initial pay-for-chore offer, Child must first begin with a tone of **humility**, as we all know Child being a member of the family means that he has an obligation to help out, regardless of compensation. Starting the conversation with humility demonstrates that he's approaching the negotiation with both careful consideration and maturity, which in turn will help him negotiate for a higher chore fee, given the tendency for a parent's willingness to pay a higher premium for chores the older a child gets. He further demonstrates his awareness of his negotiating position by **acknowledging** that while his skills may be limited, this is in all reality the *least* skilled that he would ever be in this particular job. He will naturally progress in competency, so his Parents are actually getting a bargain rate. He can then **give examples** of ways he has demonstrated accomplishments in other relevant areas to bolster his position of this being a mere stepping stone to bigger and better things. Child is quickly learning the longer the chore resume, the better the pay raise.

But it is one thing to receive a slightly higher chore fee, it is another to actually earn it. A higher pay rate demands more responsibility, so Child must establish that he has earned the right to receive higher pay by having a **go-getter** and positive attitude to his employers. Child will then **lay out**: the expected timeline for performance of the chore indicated in the initial offer; explain his business plan of when and how often he would perform the subject chores; and provide a general description of what steps would be taken with that chore to minimize future misunderstanding of the full scope of activities.

This last step may seem extreme, until one considers that taking out the trash to some rural kid may include a quarter mile trudge down the driveway after dark, or, in our case, the fact that taking out the trash is a three-step, two-day process, the first step requiring Child to guide the trash cans from their resting place and bring them to the street, carefully angling the trash cans over a series of small hills to circumvent our urban driveway that is too small for both a parked car and trash can passage, the second step being to replace the trash bag in the kitchen, and the third step of returning the cans to their rightful places the following day. To further complicate this multi-step, multi-day process, every other week is recycling or yard waste and he needs to be able to remember which week it is or at least have the wherewithal to observe what the neighbors are doing. And you thought taking out the trash was simple.

Finally, Child will **evoke empathy** to encourage Husband's acceptance of Child's counteroffer using whatever last methods he can muster: comparisons to other chore rates, previous comments by Husband about hating to do said chore, Child's maturity, age, good grades, alleged favoritism among siblings (if applicable, but risky). Child may need to go through several rounds of haggling in order to agree on negotiated terms.

H.A.G.G.L.E. for opportunities

Whether it's an opportunity for a hang out, family vacation input, or general activity, Child can use his burgeoning negotiating tactics on influencing family fun. Although opportunities to play and go on sweet vacations are dependent on his Parents' ability to create those opportunities through hard work and basic economics, Child's privilege of being a singleton means the Parents likewise don't have to spend as much time saving for vacations and deciphering interesting activities for a wide age range.

While potential opportunities are seemingly endless, Child has learned to curate his requests based on my less-than-subtle unwillingness to be inconvenienced and my distrust of other children in general. Forget enrolling Child in multiple activities just to satisfy some vague sense of cultural exposure or humble brag to others on my ability to manage an over-scheduled calendar. Forget a self-initiated outing to my personal nightmare: indoor-multi-room-sensory-overload-play-everything-places; the likely result being me crumbling into the fetal position on the sticky floor, lights glaring, children shrieking, chaos and viruses[27] everywhere.[28] Activities had to be enjoyable for the entire family.

When haggling for an opportunity to do something fun, Child begins the conversation with **humility**, as he is well aware that he is not the one to actually fund this particular activity / drive to the destination / manage scheduling. Depending on the context, he may **acknowledge** that while the hoped-for activity may be more expensive / complicated / ambitious than what would normally be suggested, he can **give examples** of ways this activity would not only benefit each individual family member, but bring added depth to the overall family experience.

---

[27] I am admittedly never concerned about the disease as much as I am about the sheer inconvenience of it.

[28] Child was able to go to these sorts of places for the occasional birthday party, as in that scenario the host family was in charge of managing the chaos.

Child then continues to make his argument by establishing he's a **go-getter** and willing to do anything to make this decision and activity easier for his parents to agree to. Clean up his room? Give him a gold medal, because he has just set a personal best in room tidying time. Chores not completed? Either they are quickly finished or he may offer other privileges as collateral to buy more time (e.g., no screen time until X chore is completed). To seal the deal, Child then will **lay out** the expected timeline for how to execute this activity and its ensuing influence on the rest of the calendar.

At this point, either one or two things will happen. In the first scenario, Child's argument will have been so successful that the Parent agrees to the activity before getting to the final H.A.G.G.L.E. step. In this case, Child could **evoke empathy** by acknowledging the Parent's contribution to this opportunity and emphasize the positive aspects of it. In the second scenario, the Parent may be still dithering on whether to grant the request. In that case, Child will **evoke empathy** by reminding the Parent of how much the missed opportunities of childhood freedom and play dates still haunt them to this day and how often they are still brought up as deeply personal regrets. If Child is still not successful, well, then he can recall his earlier lesson on being R.E.A.L. in the face of failure: **reflect** on what happened; **evaluate** what can be improved in his next activity selection; **act to correct** any deficiencies in his attempt to H.A.G.G.L.E.; **look over results** of his after-action review and attempt again.

CHAPTER XII
C.H.O.I.C.E.

Early in our marriage Husband and I would choose which movie to watch through a two-step process: (i) Designated Person #1 picks three DVDs from our selection; (ii) Designated Person #2 chooses one DVD from that limited option. This worked mostly well because we were two reasonable adults and had generally similar tastes in film. Child is now old enough to play along with us (although on streaming), but we don't trust him enough to give him Designated Person #1 privilege.

Independent choice making falls into two buckets: (i) Having the wisdom to make a good choice and (ii) having the fortitude to move forward in that choice.

The first bucket is one where most parents focus, especially in the early stages of training. The art of choice is a delicate dance of sharing experience as a parent and enabling your children to make the choice (right or wrong) themselves. Failure is inevitable, so why not have them fail when they're still wearing the training wheels of life?

Having choices in fact demonstrates the privilege that we live in. From the spectrum of choosing clothing or extracurriculars to choosing what political party we subscribe, billions of individuals don't get these opportunities. Celebrate the opportunity to have choices in life.

Many well-meaning parents try to shield their child (and themselves) from facing an uncomfortable situation. But while your child may go through life unscathed, you've also created an eventual basement dweller. In fact, the ability to make a choice is as much on training parents as it is on children.

Now one doesn't always have the luxury of having multiple options to allow for a choice. Just like being on a cross-country road trip and the only available restaurant is fast food, buckling down and making the best of what you're given is also a necessary and admirable trait. However, if the prospect of allowing your child to make an independent choice unreasonably terrifies you, I've created a succinct illustration of the overall choice strategy we've given Child, which will blend the art of meeting short term goals while effecting long-term strategy.

When giving your child a C.H.O.I.C.E., try to:

Construct the scenario.

Hold your opinion

Okay to ask guiding questions

Illustrate analytical reasoning

Champion child's decision ownership

Encourage future application

Construct the scenario

Naturally, I am opinionated about a lot of things. My completely unbiased observations show many parents stay in the red herring stage of choice creation way too long. What I mean by this statement is parents will often give their children small decisions to make, which is a great start. But it's also a distraction. These choices aren't enough to encourage personal decision-making growth. And children need the opportunity to learn about choices and think through the consequences sooner than we tend to believe they are.

Many parent-directed choices will begin as simply as choosing which ice cream to buy (my favorite choice because it's ice cream and I can still buy the one I want regardless), or a shirt style to wear. As early as I could remember I would choose to wear pink over all other colors. If pink was not available, red as its closest cousin was the reluctant option. One school year I chose to grow out my bangs, and twenty-five years later my family still brings up the trauma of my daily complaining and tears with awkward, half-grown hair that everyone else had to endure. These choices (minus the bangs), were simple. They teach a little about the consequences of choice; that once a choice is made, then one will need to live with it.

While we're on that topic, I also want to take a moment to share the other opinion I have with this early choice stage. Let's return to the ice cream scenario: Child and I are at our fabulously delicious local ice cream parlor-gas station[29] and he decides that he wants to try the Blue Moo flavor and I want a very-adult Peanut Butter Swirl. He makes his choice, I make mine, and after paying for our ice cream, we dig in. But two bites in, Child decides he doesn't want his Blue Moo. He doesn't like it as much as he would like the Peanut Butter Swirl. He asks to switch. What do you, as a parent, do: switch or stay?

Very few opportunities in life allow do-overs, and especially do-overs without lingering consequences such as debt or lost time, for added complexity.[30] I

---

[29] Yes, it's real and don't judge it until you've had it.

[30] Besides grandchildren, which we've discussed in Chapter VI B.O.N.D.

could take him up at his offer to switch ice cream, which would give him a slightly higher amount of satisfaction for that quick five minutes that he eats it. But what if I don't switch? Child would learn that sometimes the choices we make turn out differently than expected. Child would learn resilience. Child would learn that his mother isn't going to magically solve all of his problems. Child would learn that ice cream is a small matter, and the next choices may be larger, so there should be greater care taken to weigh options. Sometimes choices work out, and sometimes they're a minor inconvenience. It's only ice cream.

Besides, I hate Blue Moo, and I also don't want to resent my child for taking away an opportunity to enjoy myself in that moment, so I decline.

Once children start becoming sentient, they quickly start asserting their own desire for making choices. Obviously, the choice that a child can be trusted to make depends on their maturity, age, cultural background, among other factors. A tired Child is a lethargic and temperamental monster, so he will not be able to choose his bedtime while he is under my roof. "Constructing a scenario" can form from two different methods:

(i) parental-directed

and

(ii) child-directed.

A parental directed scenario is one where the parent determines independently whether a situation would allow for a child to demonstrate a trait or skill that would be a growth opportunity. A child directed scenario is one that the child brings to the parent independently. The conclusion to whether the child is able to act in the relevant situation is determined in either outcome by the parent.

Fortunately for Child, my own self-concern enables Child to exercise his autonomy through scenario #1 earlier than many of his peers.

Hold your opinion

Once a child is presented with a choice, the parent should refrain from offering an opinion on what outcome they should choose. The reason is simple: Offering an opinion mid-choice is the same as telling your child what to do. They don't have a choice. They don't go through the mental work of thinking through the choice and its consequences. They essentially become dogs. Don't short-change your child with this.

Child is very set in his ways when it comes to what he wants to wear. Little does he know, he inherited that trait from me. Even as a baby, Child refused to wear any of the adorable hats that all of the other compliant babies wore. I quickly realized the futility of that battle. He has also spent most of his life wearing a borderline-inappropriate amount of clothing. Child was born with a fully operating internal furnace, so wearing anything other than a diaper and a onesie usually resulted in heat rash. Heat rash was uncomfortable, not to mention unsightly. Aesthetics demanded minimal clothing, and Child was eager to comply. The minimal-clothing trend continued until Child became aware that he could express a choice with his clothing (and lack of it). As such, by the time he was old enough to go to kindergarten, he refused to wear anything other than shorts.

When Child made it clear he did not want to wear anything other than shorts, I was not in favor of that decision. I, of course, having read the parent handbook and dress code, was aware that pants were required after a certain temperature change. And failure to follow that rule would result in consequences such as not being allowed to go to recess or (horror!) a note home to the parent.

Child being more of a rebel than I ever was or am, wasn't fazed at the consequences. I, on the other hand, was hanging on by a thread due to a new job, Husband's second deployment, and a temperamental youth. Challenging an institution's shorts policy was low on my priority list. But I decided to give it a try. And I held my opinion. For a few weeks while the weather turned colder and November inched closer, I began to think we were in the clear. Until one day, when The Note came home. The Note gently but firmly advised me that the six-year-old needed to wear pants due to the colder temperatures. And failure to wear pants would result in escalating measures, beginning with Child not being allowed to go outside to recess.

I am a coward, so I sat down and basically let Child know the grand experiment was over and I would be wresting control over his clothing choice. Of course, this was more out of concern for the teacher's well-being from not getting a break from a high-energy singleton than actually following the rules. At least that is what I tried to tell myself. So, I gave in to the demands. Child fitfully wore pants November through February that school year.

Okay to ask guiding questions

Guiding questions are training wheels. Once children have the exposure and practice of thinking through a logic chain on their own, guiding questions will be fewer. Of course, the discerning parent who practices guiding questions must also take care to not unduly influence the question asked. As any pollster knows, answers can be easily manipulated based on the initial questions asked. Questions should be framed as neutrally as possible to encourage maximum child engagement. You can tell you're getting through with effective questions when their eyes begin to glaze over. That means they're thinking.

Guiding questions are intended to guide the child from short-term reasoning into long-term reasoning as the child ages. Children have a very hard time perceiving the future, because to a child, the world started when they were born and the free ride is going to last forever.

Child may be in elementary school, but for several years we've tried to instill in him the view that the choices he makes now with learning how to effectively study and persevering even when the subject is hard or boring will pay dividends once he goes to middle and high school. I don't think he's been entirely convinced, but I figured that repeating this enough will implant a false memory so that he will think it was all his idea and actually follow through.

Despite the failure of his Shorts Only experiment during kindergarten, Child wasn't swayed in first grade. As fall began to wind down and the thirty-degree daily swings of Midwestern transition weather began, Child once again began to lobby to wear shorts year-round. Lobbying grew increasingly furtive as winter approached. As decision time drew nearer, I began to ask Child guiding questions to try to get him to think through his initial position:

"What happens if you're cold at school but you don't have more clothes to put on?"

"What happens if the teacher won't let you go outside?"

I tried very hard to guide Child to the convenient answer. Child didn't budge.

Illustrate analytical reasoning

From the simplest to the most complex scenario, a choice can be reduced to an if-then statement. "If I choose X, then Y may happen." Children are not necessarily equipped with the powers of deduction, so parents supplement with guiding questions to illustrate the logic chain related to their choice. It's a simple yet critical aspect to teach children about choices and their ensuing consequences.

When Child was old enough to navigate the playground but young enough to still ask for help, I created a rule that if he can get himself up to a ledge, ladder, etc., then he would need to get himself down. The reasons behind this were twofold: First, he would be forced to consider whether or not the object he was about to climb on could be feasibly negotiated. Child was too young to understand the full potential of this exercise, so consistent with his age of development I kept it simple and made it a rule. A rule that he would have to think about. Unlike many of those you may encounter in the workforce, Child was learning the skill of thinking before acting.

Second, if I was in the middle of a conversation with the one mom I could somehow magically relate to at the park, I didn't want that socialization opportunity to die from fielding incessant pleas for help. Frequent interruptions would result in no more park visits. And an enjoyable park experience was in everyone's best interest.

This climbing rule has persisted for almost a decade. And other than offering encouragement when Child doubted his ability to descend, I've never had to fully engage in a rescue. Now that he's old enough to run around the 'hood by himself or with his friends, I trust him more and worry less. He's had a decade of experience with fraughtful situations and has outmaneuvered them all. And as Child grows older, the previously imposed rules move more into actual choices and related expectations for increased analytical reasoning.

Returning to Child's ongoing shorts campaign, previously guiding questions led by Mother transitioned into "if-then" statements offered by Child.

"If I wear shorts, then I could be kept from outside recess."
"If I am cold, then I will not have more clothes to put on."

I offered one "if-then" statement of my own: *"If Child complains of being cold, then Child will not be allowed to wear shorts again."*

He was willing to roll the dice. October transitioned into November and still no pants (and no Note). Maybe the first graders were broken in enough to not be as carefully scrutinized. Maybe the teachers could see that Child was adapting to the cold environment by growing a thick carpet of leg hair over the fall. Either way, no Note came home in first grade and Child left winter victorious.

Champion child's decision ownership

Positive reinforcement is the strongest motivator for most, and children are no exception. Championing your child's ownership of the decisions they make will encourage future good decisioning. Academics are extremely important, so I spend a lot of time understanding what Child is learning at school, where his weaknesses are, re-explaining concepts in a way that may be more aligned with his thought process, and enforcing study time. I also heap excessive amounts of praise on him when he does well so that he stays motivated to continue making positive academic choices. Pushing academic diligence early is like saving for retirement. Hit it hard in the beginning and reap the advantages of the compounding interest of quality study habits and knowledge acquisition by the time they hit high school, when it really matters. No amount of cramming will help get the grades Child needs to do what he wants in life.

Child recently confided in me that one of his teachers rewards As on tests with candy. I'm not opposed to that strategy—after all, who of us hasn't gone for a food reward? How that is not motivation enough to do well, I have no idea, as I still have to nag him to study. Don't worry if you're too enlightened to perpetuate the obesity rate of children in the Midwest; feel free to choose other methods. Sometimes a constant yet gentle reminder that they almost missed out on a fun play date (or "hang out" as I was later corrected to say) due to a messy room is enough.

Child loves a challenge, and nothing is more challenging than facing a finite amount of time and a growing list of things to get done. Intro Child's ultra-frenemy, the Checklist. As Master Yoda said, "Do or do not. There is no try." The Checklist is really a love-hate relationship as it is per se objective. As a burgeoning young man of responsibility, Child can use the Checklist to understand the expectations set on him and make the choice to action them. Choosing to delay and avoid means he does not get to enjoy potential hang outs (a small, socially intertwined community means play dates can happen within the span of a few minutes), watch YouTube or enjoy other prepubescent perquisites. Make the choice to satisfy the Checklist chores, and he's as free as an off-leash puppy in a dog park.

Before anyone starts to wonder if we derive some sort of sick parental pleasure from seeing how much can be piled on the Checklist, know that I have an interest in Child fulfilling his chores as well. While I can't show all my cards, my happiness is largely entwined with Child's. If he's off and larking about with his friends, I get more me time. It's another win-win and a strong incentive for fairness.

Encourage future application

While we mostly addressed bucket #1 (Having the wisdom to generally make good choices), Child's fortitude to move forward in that choice (bucket #2) enabled him to experience something that typical seven-year-olds couldn't. Child and I went on a family trip with my parents, my siblings, and their spouses. Although it wasn't winter, the weather was cold enough to need a jacket and several layers of clothing and it was windy. We stayed together at a house within walking distance to a rocky beach and my brother and brothers-in-law wanted to prove their manliness by jumping into the frigid water. Child, not wanting to be left out, wanted to join them. Given Child's fortitude with cold in the past, I asked him a few probing questions and once satisfied, let him proceed.

The wind blew steady, brushing those of us too close to the water with cold mist. The humidity in the air caused the temperature to seem colder than it supposedly was, with many of us layered in jackets and long sleeves. The waves careened with measured force onto the beach and the twilight of the evening blended rocky sand, sea, and sky into complementary shades of grey. Child and his uncles quickly undressed to their swim trunks, with Child barely able to hide his excitement at the prospect of venturing into the frigid waters.

Hunched slightly against the wind, Child grasped the hand of his eldest uncle and practically skipped into the waves. The initial shock of the water only slightly slowed him as he waded into the water up to his torso. He stayed for several minutes, jumping, laughing, and emanating the joy most of us aspire to have at some point of our lives, while the rest of the group looked on. After a few minutes that seemed longer in person, Child turned back to the beach and bounded up from the water with exuberance. I was very proud. And I secretly figured if Child had the mental fortitude to willingly enter sixty-degree water, he would have the tenacity to do anything.

The beauty of experience with making choices, and particularly with making good choices, is that experience constantly grows. The more experience Child has of analyzing a situation, making a positive choice, and following through with said choice, the more likely he will continue to follow the pattern.

Five years after his initial kindergarten experiment, Child is still sticking with his pants boycott. He considers it a point of pride to have been able to count on one hand the number of times he wore pants during the school year and has influenced other young men to follow suit. Given his tenacity, the only times he has relegated to wearing pants for more than an hour are: skiing (Child), winter polar vortex[31] (Mother) and Christmas formal dinner (Mother).

---

[31] That is, assuming he's going outside. He's still in shorts and mostly shirtless inside. And no, I am not one of those people that cranks up the heat. I care about my money and the environment too much.

CHAPTER XIII
Parting W.I.S.D.O.M.

Parenting is difficult. Especially with young children. And unfortunately, it doesn't get easier. Although, full disclosure, I really appreciate the ages of five to ten. It's incredibly interesting to see how Child has grown as a person, including the quality of his character and his relative-to-age accomplishments. He's become someone we can joke with, appreciate music together, actively plan for the future, and allow a parental swear word to escape, albeit with a 25-cent penalty to Child's swear jar (easiest fine I've ever paid). I'm hopeful that we get a few more years of fun in before puberty and tough life choices start to make things serious.

I initially wanted to create a book that mothers like me could enjoy and find a reprieve from incessant and oftentimes contradictory parenting dogma. But while this book is a fantastic way to avoid the overly flowery and exhaustingly emotional take many other mommy-hood books play on, this book does have its limits. And unfortunately, raising a new human thing means you're simultaneously also uncovering your own repressed memories and failed personal expectations.

I recently came across a pre-formatted school year journal I received as a gift during my late elementary years. The journal began in Kindergarten and went through eighth grade. Surprisingly, I managed to fill out about two-thirds of the pages. If only my track record stayed consistent in my adult years. Each school year had sections where you could list your best friends, favorite subjects, and what you wanted to be when you grew up. For several years I consistently documented three potential career paths, which coincidentally began with As: archeologist (Indiana Jones was a severe hottie and even at ten years old I could see that), astronaut (Major Nelson—

also hot) and author (no hotties that I knew of here, I just liked to read).

I excitedly brought the journal to Child as he sat quietly doing his homework. Happy for the sanctioned distraction, he set aside his assignment and began to turn the pages of my purple-inked entries. Curious as to what his own mother was like at his age, he flipped the journal to fourth grade and began to quietly read. Not even two seconds after finishing my career aspirations entry, he laid the book on his lap, looked critically at me and promptly quipped, "But you're none of those." Well thank you, Child. But attorney starts with an A, so there. In some ways, this book was a desire to make Child proud.[32]

While we can't change our past, we can also choose to move forward and remake our future. Don't be like an unnamed and unfortunate member of the public who I overheard blaming her addiction to cigarettes

---

[32]In a separate but related conversation, Child and I were discussing my book and I asked him if he would be proud of me. He responded, a glint of mischief in his eye, "Why would I be proud of you if you don't have any sales?" Child is my harshest critic.

on her mother not breastfeeding her enough. That amount of personal deflection will do nothing but cause us to stagnate.

Our failures don't define our future

Our unofficial family motto is: Even a blind squirrel finds an acorn every now and then. And our family slogan is: Above Average. Don't ask me what the difference between a motto and slogan is, just know that there is one. More importantly, both quotes are self-evident of our respective families' two hundred years of voting "Present" while meandering throughout the Midwest-South-Appalachia regions. With no history of multi-generational wealth or influence to speak of, we're still hopeful that this next generation will be the one to change the narrative.

Perhaps driven by family history, or perhaps aware of my own inadequacies, I Marshmallow-Tested Child when he was around three years old. The Marshmallow Test is a psychological experiment originally led by psychologist Walter Mischel at Stanford University in 1970 to study delayed gratification.[33] The Marshmallow Test went as follows: a child, usually between the ages of three to seven, was seated at a table and presented with a single marshmallow. The proctor told the child that if they didn't eat the marshmallow right away, they would receive another marshmallow in fifteen minutes. The study then analyzed what children would do to pass the time to distract themselves, or how long the subject would wait until succumbing to temptation. The hypothesis of the test was that children who exhibited self-discipline were going to be more successful in life. Whether or not this remains to be a valid psychological test, when I read about this test, I immediately knew I needed to Marshmallow Test Child.

I sat Child at the kitchen table and placed a large, white, and puffy marshmallow on a plate in front of him. I carefully explained to Child that he could eat the marshmallow now, or if he waited, he could have more marshmallows. Child, only three and still not quite understanding everything that I would tell him,

---

[33] Conti, Regina. "Delay of Gratification." Encyclopedia Britannica. https://www.britannica.com/science/delay-of-gratification#ref12 06154. Accessed June 12, 2020.

seemed to consent. I quietly left the room, but stayed behind the kitchen door to silently watch him from behind the cracked door. The minutes painfully crept by and I wished I had my own marshmallow. I observed Child sit quietly, hands flat on the table, and looking around the room, seemingly to distract himself. As the minutes progressed, he began to move his hands around the table top, kick his legs, and take furtive glances at the marshmallow in front of him. Another minute passed and he began to play with the marshmallow, batting it around like a cat. At the five-minute mark, the temptation proved too great. He raised the marshmallow to his mouth and took a giant bite. The rest quickly followed.

I wanted to Marshmallow Test Child in order to gauge his natural sense of self-control. To me, self-control and delayed gratification have been the largest contributing factors to any perceived successes I've had. I'm not particularly smart or gifted, especially in areas that actually matter, but as a positive side effect of my lack of social cues, I'm also able to persistently stay on a difficult course by shutting off my emotions and believing that the momentary pain wouldn't kill me. This will of course work only up until the point where the activity does actually kill me, but I haven't gotten that far yet.

I tried not to let Child's Marshmallow Test failure disappoint me too much. But it did. I tried to take comfort in the fact that he was on the young end of the experimental subjects and probably lacked the psychological maturity for success, even if he had understood what I was trying to do. I admitted to having overreached on this matter, despite previous successes in buying toys, supplemental educational workbooks or playing games that were one to two years more advanced at Child's age at the time. I didn't care about the actual Marshmallow Test. I was concerned that he lacked the self-control he would need to get through life. I didn't Marshmallow Test him again. But I continued to train and emphasize the virtues of delaying gratification and self-control, out of fear he would devolve into some sort of emotion-driven vagrant.

Four years later, Child entered second grade. In order to rally the students to good behavior, his classroom teacher created a point system where the children could earn points based on attendance, homework completion, listening, and other positive social activities. These points could then be redeemed for a variety of prizes, ranging from candy, to pencils, to stickers, to gift cards and other enticing tchotchkes. The pièce de résistance of potential prizes was a bobblehead of the jovial, handle-bar mustachioed Mr. Redlegs mascot of the Cincinnati Reds, piloting a Star Wars X-wing fighter. At a steep price of 250 points, it would take an enterprising young child most of the school year to accumulate the amount of points needed to reach that level. The Reds X-wing had been waiting in the teacher's prize closet for over two years to be redeemed. This prize combined two of Child's most fervent interests at that time. Child had to have it.

Starting in October, Child began to save his classroom points. While other students were buying weekly treats and living precariously on zero-sum spending budgets, Child resisted. He slowly began to see his classroom points begin to accumulate and every week would give Husband and me an update on how many points he had earned and held. The weeks and months slowly ticked by. Child and I would periodically calculate how many more points he needed to earn in order to redeem his prize by the end of the school year. Child became as invested in not losing points for anti-social behavior as he did in earning them. He became addicted to watching his points accumulate in his account, similar to what adults experience when we finally start investing in our retirement accounts, although his teacher's model didn't incorporate compound interest calculations. Finally, in April, just three weeks shy of the end of the school year, Child earned his 250 points.

He was of course excited to earn his coveted prize. Husband and I were even more excited about his extraordinary showing of self-control. Six months can seem impossibly long for adults, much less for a child. Every week he was faced with the temptation to spend his points on the immediately gratifying smaller prizes he could earn at that moment. His decision to earn the Reds X-wing was entirely his own. Even though he failed the Marshmallow Test, it didn't mean that he was a failure. Husband and I kept encouraging self-control and Child somehow listened. I also learned an important lesson over this six-month time period. Child taught me that even though we may not perform as we would hope initially, we don't have to give up. We can still try. And I have to believe that long term persistence will pay out in the end.

We can create our own balance

Work-life balance is especially complicated for women who work outside of the home.

First, what is *work*? Is it just your career? Or does it include child rearing? I cynically count *work* as basically everything that I do that is both uncomfortable and has an end-goal, which means 95% of my existence is considered work. This includes taking the three minutes to prepare dinner by opening the door to the freezer, removing the first frozen item that is deemed a meal (ice cream still counts, if I could be completely honest, but likely it's a lasagna), noisily peeling the film surrounding the frozen tray, and dumping it unceremoniously in a still-heating oven, while compensating for the imprecise heating by adding an extra five minutes to the suggested cooking time. I do this because I have a legal obligation to feed my minor, who let's be honest, probably would prefer ice cream anyway.

Other things count as work, even if not legally required. After successive "no's," I should agree to do something Child wants to do, so I reluctantly agree to play a board game with him because it's hot, and I'd rather not go outside in the irrepressibly sweltering Midwestern humidity.[34] Sadly, even one of my favorite pastimes has become fetid with the stink of obligation. Since realizing that I only have ten more years to train to run as fast as I possibly can before fighting the inevitable decline, I've found myself struggling through hilly and humid runs that I'm also somehow supposed to be pacing aggressively. Endorphins are supposed to make you happy, but

---

[34] The Midwest is not the South, so the heat and humidity we face isn't taken as seriously by anyone outside of our region, but it's still incredibly oppressive. I can imagine any of my Southern friends who are reading this will simply respond with, "*Bless your heart.*"

somehow this has caused even more anxiety. I give you permission to admit you feel the same.

Second, by extension, what is classified as *life* in this question of work-life balance? Is it everything outside of your career? Is it solely the things that you find personally fulfilling? Is it simply being able to adapt the time needed to be with your family? Or is it a subset of everything, including work?

For me, it's the latter because, honestly, there are things that I like and I don't like in each of these situations. I don't like dealing with arrogant colleagues that I somehow am supposed to collaborate with, but I do like using my education and occasionally-lucid arguments of persuasion to resolve a pressing matter at my work. I don't like having to contribute to household mediocrities, like heating frozen food or vacuuming, but I do like having a house that Marie Kondo would say, "sparks joy." I don't like realizing that I've overcommitted myself and having to carefully vet the organizations I choose to give my time to, but I like being seen as an integral and reliable partner of a few groups. Regardless of what my preferences are, these are all uniquely personal positions that we must allow ourselves to confidently own without shame.

This balance between work and life will constantly change depending on the stage of life we are in with our child(ren). Early in my law career, I read an article about the elusive work-life balance of a young female attorney struggling as a law firm associate.[35] This young attorney had young children at home, so she was constantly struggling between the pull of the billable hour siren and the responsibilities with her offspring. She happened to meet up with an older female partner in the elevator[36] and the two began discussing their respective weekends. While cycling through that weekend's agenda, the elder partner mentioned that she had baked a pie. The associate was aghast. How did she have time to do this? Well, she didn't have young children and she had several associates reporting to her (see Chapter VI B.O.N.D., Delegate), so it was indeed possible.

---

[35] I have googled extensively for this article, but I can't find it.

[36] I don't really remember if it was in an elevator or not because I still haven't found the article, but I'm using my imagination to create a better picture for the reader.

The moral I took away from the story was that life will eventually become enjoyable. At the time of reading, I was facing starting my career working in a corporation rather than in a firm, which meant that I had better flexibility, but with a soon-to-be deployed husband and a five-year-old, the space created by a work-free weekend would be consumed by a lot of heavy emotional lifting and family responsibilities. Maybe my conclusion was not quite what the article was going for, but I found comfort in remembering I would eventually have a life again.

We can change how we perceive our limits

Simultaneously with the growth of our children, we parents continue to grow as people. For those who are already ingrained in child-life, it's never too late to reassess where we are, what we want to accomplish, and expand into uncharted territory.

Nine years ago, I mistakenly thought I could only do two out of three activities:

(i) have a career,

(ii) have a family and

(iii) train for a marathon.

All of them take an enormous amount of time, effort and required full-family buy-in. During Child's Year Zero I proved to myself that having a family and training for a marathon were possible. After that, I slowly transitioned to working part time, then starting law school, and eventually launching my career. For seven years I only managed having a career and having a family. Once the stress of the school routine, my work schedule, and general living became manageable, adding marathon training to the mix didn't seem insurmountable.

Training for my second marathon was both easier and more difficult than my first. At seven years old, Child was too big for a stroller. So rather than bringing him along, I had to time runs to either happen while Husband was home, use Child's sports practices as surrogate babysitting, or run one mile laps up and down the heavily-inclined sidewalk directly in front of our house. Despite desperately trying to tell myself differently, an early-thirties body is not quite as resilient as a mid-twenties, so my aptitude for injury had dramatically increased since my first marathon. In the positive, I now had access to cross-training at my work gym and the accountability of a once-weekly running group to keep me motivated to train. Sixteen weeks of training later, I completed my second marathon. And with this second accomplishment, I knew I could continue to pursue these three activities.

At the time I completed my second marathon, I did not think I could introduce more commitments to my life. But again, as the discomfort of managing these three initial activities became more routine, other conceivable activities emerged. A few years ago, my mother-in-law and I received gift certificates for a pie-making class as a Christmas present. The woman who directed us through the extremely technical process of mixing, cooling, timing, and forming dough was thorough and terrifying. She had no problem correcting missteps in over-mixing or measuring without scientific precision. I loved it.

From then on, I became the self-appointed pie baker for the family, although for years I could only manage to bake pies twice a year because it was a lengthy process; I didn't want to invest in the proper equipment to make it faster; and other priorities took precedence. Five years into my career, and Child becoming ten years old and relatively independent, I gained the time to expand my pie baking from twice a year, to making pies for multiple events during the holiday season, including an inaugural corporate bake-off.

I was determined to submit a competitive pie because I equated winning the bake-off as a surrogate victory for my real job and soothe my paralyzing inferiority I felt compared to the other attorneys.[37] I strategized that while pie was somewhat controversial (pie was the lowest ranked dessert for Husband and Child), most individuals seem to appreciate and recognize its complexity and effort. I made two pies in hopes to appeal to the widest variety of tastes: an apple pie, for the traditionalists, and a chocolate bourbon pie to

---

[37] I will admit this inferiority complex is likely self-perceived and does not necessarily reflect actual reality. Yay imposter syndrome!

appeal to the alcoholism plaguing the legal industry. Competition was fierce, as over thirty contestants vied for the top vote. Voters were split on the chocolate bourbon, but the apple pie won the day. The giant trophy with chef's hat applique now sits conspicuously over my work desk.

And I got "sweet cred" from Child for having an actual trophy.

A pie would have been impossible for me to bake two years ago. Likewise, I couldn't have devoted the effort to volunteering with various community groups that I can now commit to. For almost ten years, the thought would have been too overwhelming to attempt. If this is how you're feeling, take comfort that you are completely normal.

No matter the stage of life you're in now, remember that this is your own Marshmallow Test. Focus on what you want to do and where you want to be in the long-term. You and I are neither special nor particularly lucky. Whatever gratifying experiences we hope to enjoy in the future will eventually happen with hard work and sacrifice.

Try to do your best in the short-term. Give yourself permission to be disappointed with inevitable failures. But don't let disappointment distract your future efforts. Move on with resilience if meeting a goal doesn't happen as successfully as you would have preferred. There are very few times in life where another race can't be attempted again, another promising job opportunity doesn't pop up, another volunteer activity won't be scheduled, or another youth sports game won't be played. Parenthood and personal growth are all about the long term.

We will find success

First, great job hanging on to the end of this book. Seriously. Despite being an avid reader for twenty plus years, after finishing law school I couldn't read anything more complicated than a Reddit post outside of work because I lacked the stamina. You clearly are even more prepared to succeed than I ever was.

Second, and I don't say this lightly, be confident you will succeed not only in your own personal growth, but as a parent. It's both intimidating and discouraging to read about individuals who are exceptional. Maybe I'm just projecting my own insecurities, but I compare myself to everyone, whether it's with a career, hobby, or even how we engage with our families. I see how others have mastered their areas and see nothing but how I've failed at my own attempts. Rather than dwelling on ways past generations could have or should have done more to improve the next generation's prospects, my hope is to exponentially build on the generational P.R.I.V.I.L.E.G.E. we enjoy and help others achieve the same.

Finally, if you don't remember anything else from this book (although I hope you do, because I've worked very hard on it), just remember one phrase—with yourself, your children, and the environment, you will do **N.O. H.A.R.M.**:

No one is an island. Use your resources and realize your limits.

Own your foibles. Understand them and seek to improve.

Harness your desire to influence. Figure out just one principle you would like to impart on your child and do that. Everything else is a bonus.

Aspire to be the best. It doesn't matter if you get there, but you'll get farther than just staying as you are.

Rest assured, that even if you feel like you're failing you're not. Kids are resilient. You're doing ok.

Make yourself a priority. Don't negotiate with tiny terrorists.

Bonus Questionnaire.

For those of you who have overcommitted yourself to the point of needing a daily pep talk just to make it through a Tuesday, or are actually reading this in a book club,[38] you're in luck! I've created this supplemental questionnaire where you can share the

---

[38] My ideal book club would be about five individuals all reading different books at different speeds and just talking about what they've read. I see nothing but upside: There's no requirement to read to a certain point; no pressure to think of a unique comment to share despite three other people having discussed the passage before you; no risk of having to commit to a book that you end up hating but are stuck with, because you can decide to stop and start another one that looks better; you can learn quickly about other books you may not have originally picked out, but become interesting based on your fellow readers' experiences. There is a risk of spoilers in this model, but the benefits outweigh the risks in my opinion.

morsels[39] of W.I.S.D.O.M. and easily apply them to your own circumstances.

CHAPTER I E.G.O.I.S.M.

1. When did you first discover you wanted to be (or didn't want to be) a mother?

2. What childhood activities clued you in to how you would be or act as an adult?

3. Do you feel like your life has been on the same time table as others?

4. Finish this sentence: "Dogs are _____ _____ than human children."

CHAPTER II Overcoming P.T.S.D.

1. What is your best technique for hiding candy wrappers or other illicit paraphernalia?

2. What was the most rage-inducing assumption about your culture's treatment of pregnancy?

---

[39] "Morsels" makes me think of semi-sweet chocolate morsels that I used to sneak carefully into the kitchen to steal when I was young until I was too-old-to know better. The picture always looked better than the taste. In contrast, these W.I.S.D.O.M. morsels are just as good in real life as they appear on the page.

3. Name one misperception you had about early parenthood and how you discovered that perception gap.

4. List two ways you will give yourself grace as you experience the negative consequences of pregnancy or remember how you felt during pregnancy and list one way that you will help others in those situations.

CHAPTER III L.E.T. G.O.

1. Describe the most ridiculous baby-related item that was ever marketed to you.

2. What purchases have you secretly (or not secretly) judged others on?

3. How did your baby item purchase philosophy change from pre-pregnancy to post-pregnancy to multi-baby (if applicable)?

4. What do you wish you would have rather bought for yourself instead of spending on a child?

CHAPTER IV C.O.P.E.

1. How does control manifest most frequently in your life? Is it with work? Parenting?

Yourself? Has this changed depending on the life stage you are in?

2. What is something you have a lot of discipline in? Have you been able to use this discipline in other areas?

3. Looking back to when you were a child, what are some things that you now realize that may have been incredibly stressful points in your parents' lives but you were completely clueless about?

4. Do you think the idea of perfection is really about being perfect or is it about something else, such as having enough time to do things that you feel are important, or raising kids a different way than you would naturally do, or observing someone else's perceived successes?

<u>CHAPTER V Be S.M.A.R.T.</u>

1. In the eyes of your children or colleagues, do they know that you exist as your own independent person needing to detach and/or take time to relax?

2. What is one accomplishment you have been able to achieve in spite of the difficulty it took to get there?

3. In what subtle or not-subtle ways do you try to thwart cultural expectations?

4. When is the last time you were really honest with a friend about a life struggle?

CHAPTER VI B.O.N.D.

1. What are some of the boundaries that you have established with your family? Is there a bucket list boundary that is likely unrealistic but would be practically orgasmic to have?

2. Do you like to share activities with others in your family or do you prefer to have your own interests? Do others in your family feel the same?

3. What is your favorite holiday tradition and which one haven't you figured out how to dump yet? How can you give yourself the gift of one less obligation this holiday season?

4. List some of the reasons why you have trouble delegating. Now write a solution or counterargument for each of them.

CHAPTER VII S.E.L.F.

1. On a scale of paint-by-numbers to M.C. Escher, how creative are you?

2. Why are mothers usually expected to bear the creative burden for the family, whether it's school, work obligations, or social situations? Do you think this is changing?

3. What is the most extreme act you've taken to get some rest or get a moment away from the chaos of work or family?

4. What is the worst trash vacuum website or app for your mental health?

CHAPTER VIII Living with P.R.I.V.I.L.E.G.E.

1. Name a privilege that you may have only recently noticed that you enjoy. What was the reason for this latent realization?

2. What are some benefits that you have enjoyed thanks to your parents?

3. Are there certain privileges you experienced that you are purposefully not passing on to your children? Why or why not?

4. How have you helped others using the privileges you have experienced?

CHAPTER IX P.A.T.T.E.R.N.

1. What patterns of behavior did you and your child (or you and your parent) engage in during childhood that still carry over today?

2. How have you exploited observed patterns for your own personal gain?

3. What is your parenting magnum opus?

CHAPTER X Be R.E.A.L.

1. What are some ways that you've failed to live up to your mother-in-law's expectations?

2. How were you able to turn around your greatest failures into positive outcomes?

3. Do you think the concept of failure is overrated? How should we change the way failure is seen?

4. What is something that you're glad you failed at?

CHAPTER XI H.A.G.G.L.E.

1. When was the first time you remember negotiating for something?

2. How do you think this next generation of females are faring when it comes to negotiating?

3. What is your haggling secret weapon?

4. Who is the best negotiator you know and what makes them so good at it?

CHAPTER XII C.H.O.I.C.E.

1. If you could have an impossible do-over, what would it be?

2. At what age was or is your child mature enough to walk three blocks to a friend's house unchaperoned?

3. How has your experience with choice growing up shaped your perception of its value?

4. How old were you when you realized that choices had consequences? How did you discover this?

CHAPTER XIII Parting W.I.S.D.O.M.

1. In what ways do you fear your child or future child won't live up to your expectations? Or do you even have this as an expectation?

2. In a typical workday, if you could add one thing to make that day more personally fulfilling, what would it be? What is one thing that you would want to take away for the same reason?

3. Do you feel that you're not doing enough right now in life (whether for yourself, your family, or career)? How do you think others perceive you?

4. How do you define success?

Acknowledgements.

V—I'm sorry for being a brat. I'm trying to be better. You're hot. Thank you for spending hundreds of hours listening to my ideas, giving feedback, and basically taking this from a Google doc and making it into an actual book.

Child—You're the reason why I'm even semi-qualified to write this. I just hope that the baggage you may have from my endless harping on homework and excellence is outweighed by the enormous sense of accomplishment, fulfillment, and joy you find in life. We love you very much.

Thank you Eren, Bev, Melissa, Sue, Margaret, Susannah, and Jen for taking the time to read my manuscript and give me incredible feedback. It means a lot!

Thank you, Victoria, for your detailed approach to editing and advising me throughout this process. It was fun to work with you!

Deeter—thank you in advance for featuring me on your podcast.

Made in the USA
Monee, IL
29 January 2021

59107476R00146